The Legion
of Marching Madmen

WILLIAM JAMES BLACKLEDGE

The Legion
of Marching Madmen
Experiences of a British Soldier on
Campaign in Mesopotamia During the
First World War

W. J. Blackledge

LEONAUR

The Legion of Marching Madmen
Experiences of a British Soldier on Campaign in Mesopotamia During the
First World War
by W. J. Blackledge

First published under the title
The Legion of Marching Madmen

Leonaur is an imprint of Oakpast Ltd

ISBN: 978-1-78282-333-9 (hardcover)
ISBN: 978-1-78282-334-6 (softcover)

http://www.leonaur.com

Publisher's Notes

Contents

"What did you do in the Great War?"
It appeared by the girl's manner that this was a witticism rather than
a question.
"I was in Mesopotamia."
"Oh, you were in that picnic, were you?"
"Yes—one of the boys flogged across Asia Minor."
"Really! What an extraordinary thing to say!"

LAQAR QUF

BELED RUZ

BAGHDAD

FALUJAH

CTESIPHON

AZIZIYEH

MUSAIYIB

HANNA

KERBELA•

BABYLON

SANNAIYAT

HILLAH

KUT

M E S O P O T

•HA

NEJFE•

KUFA

DIWANIYAH

R.

SHATRA
•

EUPHRATES

SAMAWA

SYRIAN

NASIRIYEH

DESERT

Railways existing before War 1914-1919 +++++
built by British up to Nov 11ᵗʰ 1918 + + + + +

SCALE OF MILES

0   50   100   150

CHAPTER 1

My Nightmare Adolescence

November, 1914.—We land! God knows how! Appalling muddle. Scores of men drowned before my eyes as we scramble from boats to shore. No sooner on dry land than we meet terrific enfilade of fire. Men drop all around me, mown down like rotten sheep by fire of jeering Turks. Ghastly. We had not covered five hundred yards of this strange land when two companies in front line wiped out. Indians running with us and yelling excitedly. See some drop with hands clasped around bellies. Queer expressions in their dark faces. Awful slaughter. Running blindly, crouching low, tummy in sand, firing from snap. It seemed an age—running head down towards that hail of lead. Could not see. Maybe I closed my eyes. It was horrible—that yelling, screams of pain, rattle of fire. Chattering machine guns raked us with hot lead. I was sick. Hundreds dropping in those terrible minutes. Dead lying around in heaps. Stumbling over them. Felt a coward. Wanted to stop one so I could get it over. I knew we could not survive that shower of bullets. It had to come. Mine came. A hot, stinging jab in the shoulder. Strange giddiness. Blindness. Falling. . . .

Such was my impression of the actual landing in Mesopotamia in that never-to-be-forgotten November of 1914, less than four months after the commencement of the Great War of 1914-1918.

Such was my baptism of fire. It was recorded in my diary as I lay in the improvised hospital near Basrah—the important base at the mouth of the River Tigris which was occupied by the British Force about two weeks after landing in the country.

Basrah, or Bussorah, as it is known to lovers of *The Arabian Nights*, reeks with history. It is thousands of years old, and has yielded to the sway of Saracens, Persians, Turks and Arabians. It was from this port of the Persian Gulf that Sinbad the Sailor set off on some of his voyages of discovery.

It was at this port where hundreds of British lads were slaughtered and drowned. Since I wrote those disjointed sentences in my diary much water has flowed down the Land of the Two Rivers, but I see no reason to alter a single word. Historians have written that the Mesopotamian Expeditionary Force steamed into the Persian Gulf, disembarked in boats and landed without losing a single man. It is not true. I was there. I saw whole bunches annihilated.

The official "eye-witness" of the campaign, Edmund Candler, states in his work, *The Long Road to Baghdad*, "A naval and military party landed and occupied Fao Fort and Town. The Turkish infantry, decamped at an early stage, and we did not lose a single man." But this writer is reporting from records. He makes it clear that he was not in the original landing.

General Townshend, who went into the campaign at a later date writes, in *My Campaign in Mesopotamia*, of that historic landing: "Several men were drowned in the process. . . .".

The muddle of Mesopotamia was bigger than that of any other campaign in the Great War. It was more remote, for one thing. On other fronts we profited to some extent by mistakes. In Iraq, as it is now called, we went from one blunder to another. We threw away thousands of lives. In that first crazy advance, without adequate lines of communications, we left the desert behind us strewn with dead and wounded. Hundreds of helpless men fell into the hands of lust-maddened, sadistic Arab women. I saw some of them—stripped naked, bodies blackened by the sun, horribly mutilated, tortured in that way, as I know from experience, only Arab women can torture white men.

So far as I can discover, the Mesopotamian Campaign has been recorded only by militarists, historians who never write anything "indiscreet or contrary to public policy," and political deceivers. I am not concerned with such views. Mine is the untold story—an account of what one rather young Tommy saw from the fighting line.

I was at the most impressionable age when I went through that searing experience. Mine was a nightmare adolescence. I never thought I could bring myself to tell the truth about this war. For years I have fought against any such notion. But the passing of time has not dimmed the haunting pictures. As I write, wars are still raging, fears and rumours of war occupy the public mind and conscience. It is patent to the meanest intelligence that we have not yet done with war and all its devastating rottenness. The war babies of my generation are now ripe for slaughter. My own boys are coming of fodder age. One already has his "thumbs in line with the seams of his trousers" for the greater glory of the O.T.C., and another will soon follow. I cannot do a thing about it—save tell what I know. I'll tell what I saw. I'll tell as much as a publisher dare print. I'll tell more than was ever told before.

Looking through my old diary, I know I shall find no difficulty in setting down just what happened to me and to those immediately associated with me. It all comes back. When I think of that boy who grew to manhood overnight and in the midst of that blood and lust and cheap death—I look at my own boys and hope to God there will never be another. After that landing they called me "Tiger."

But I cannot relate young Tiger's tale without bringing in Steve Barry. We met on stretchers, side by side, in that shakedown of a hospital near Basrah. There was a queer bunch of fellows there—English, Scots, Welsh, Irish, as well as Indians. Steve, however, seemed different from them all. British by birth, he had spent most of his life abroad, mainly in the United States. He talked and behaved like an American. I believe there were some Americans with the force even at that early date, but they did not come within my ken. Years later, while working among the Armenian and Assyrian refugees, I came into contact with the American Mission—but that is another story.

Because of the flies and the heat and the stench, it did not take us long to get away from that gory casualty station. Steve and I contrived to be drafted into the same company. This new-found friend knew his way about the world. He was much older than I. A regular tough *wallah*. For my part, I fancy there was considerable hero-worship in that friendship.

The next phase came when we found ourselves marching with the column advancing on Kurna. On account of its position at the junction of the old Euphrates and the Tigris, this town was of great strategical importance, since its capture would give the British control of the passage to the two rivers, secure the safety of the oil wells—the *raison d'être* for the whole campaign—and also control of the navigable waterway of the Persian Gulf.

Johnny Turk knew all about its importance. We had to fight hard for it, and we soon learned to respect the enemy. Johnny Turk could fight. Our big trouble was to distinguish friend from foe among the local Arabs. They always ranged themselves on the side of the winner. So we treated them as enemies until we had taken a position.

In the advance on Kurna we had to take a desert village with an unpronounceable name like Meezra. As soon as we came within sight of the huddle of habitations we deployed into line for the charge. The Turks rose up in a sandy cloud and met us. Thereafter a perfect family scrap. We were soon at close quarters. No trench warfare this.

It was my first taste after that terrible landing. But now we were in better state and bigger numbers. So we went to it. The Turks kicked up a terrific hullabaloo. *Allah* was on every fellow's tongue. We had them at a disadvantage on that sloping ground. Men must be a bit crazy to bring off a charge like that. It was a sticky business. We were yelling and jabbing at each other like a lot of maniacs. Later in the campaign I ceased to look at it that way. It was amazing how one could adapt oneself to this cold-blooded slaughter. Individually, it was all a matter of self-defence. You had to get the other fellow before he had time to get you.

Sticking stuffed sacks in training camp had been child's play. Sticking at the belly of a dusty, sweating Turk who was also intent on sticking was—well, just a sticky mess. A bayoneted man grunts like a pig and spurts blood.

Perhaps it was by instinct that I kept by the side of Steve. He was like a big brother to me. And more than once he saved me from receiving an ugly jab. He was an old hand, knowing most of the tricks. I remember giving the jerking twist that releases the bayonet and swinging round to meet the big, black-bearded fellow who had stepped into a dead brother's shoes. I can see him now, bearing down on me, towering, fierce eyes, slavering mouth, the long bayonet making straight for my vitals—when Steve's rifle came down with a crash on the wretched devil's pate, crushing it as one would an egg shell. . . .

And all the time Steve was shouting:

"Come on, you blankety sons of *Allah!*"

He was in his element, and he could kick up as much din as any Mahommedan Turk.

Never shall I forget that charge. We were slowly forcing them back and back, jabbing and slashing, floundering and stumbling over dead and wounded—our own and those of the enemy. There would be no question of turning back. We had to take Meezra before nightfall

14

because there was a much more important job ahead. We inched our way with streaming bayonets. The grey dust rose in clouds. Sometimes there was a break in the line and we would race forward a few yards, only to be pulled up by a massed rank of glistening, sawing bayonets. Then we were at it again. And through it all I could hear Steve yelling. Occasionally he would stay his jaw tackle to bawl:

"Okay, Tiger?"

"Okay my foot!"

That answer always amused him. The Lord only knows why. But I realise now how reassuring it must have been to that young boy Tiger, a slight, rather under-sized, fair-haired fellow, to have the big, hard-bitten American bawl his query in the midst of all the heat and dust and sweat and blood of those stand-up scraps.

Again we broke the line. The section we had engaged dashed away towards a palm grove. We required no instructions to prevent them getting into shelter. We raced after them, hell for leather. We were then breaking through the farmsteads that fringed the desert village. Yelling women and barking dogs were added to the racket of battle. We stumbled among the date palms, played a deadly sort of hide and seek, picking our men and taking pot shots.

Apparently we had turned the enemy's flank. We could only guess at such things. A Tommy fights just what he can see in front of him. He cannot take cognisance of what is happening along the whole line. It appears we had cut off a bunch of Turks and had surrounded them, trapped them in this belt of palms. It was certainly more luck than good management on our part.

I note the phrase "rather glad" in my diary about this incident. I recall feeling rather glad that what we did to those tough fellows within the palm belt was somehow hidden. Would we have acted so ferociously out on the plain? I don't know. There is a beastly kind of madness that comes over one in the heat of a charge. I supposed then that we should not get out of the belt alive if we did not slaughter every man in sight.

Slaughter was correct.

Somebody cried: "Here's your meat!"

How apt! Little things like that stick in the sensitive mind. There was not a Johnny standing when we staggered out and stumbled towards the village. I remember hanging on to Steve's belt as we shuffled on through the dust. We had been hoofing for several hours before that engagement had started. I was feeling thoroughly weary and sick, and things were turning over in my stomach.

"Stop blubbering, you——!"

But even then there was that brotherly feeling in the way Steve snorted.

I started laughing.

"Who would be a soldier!" I squeaked.

"Stow that, Tiger! Stow it, I tell you!"

The next I knew we were in possession of the village of Meezra. We camped among the huddle of huts. The "friendly" Arabs were offering us of their possessions, which included their women folk. Perhaps that was how it went with Johnny Turk, but no such fare was permitted when a British force took over a town or village. Officially, women and loot were very much frowned upon, and the Tommy who was discovered at that game was likely to find himself tied to the wheel of a wagon. Just the same, many a Tommy took the risk! After all, you can't make beasts of men and then compel them to keep their thoughts clean. War is war. It means women and even children.

Guards were turned out. Somebody was calling "*Char up*" *char* being Hindustani for good Indian tea. We scrambled round the field kitchen and filled our dixie cans with the steaming fluid. It was nectar.

"Well, you li'l son of a gun, all right now?"

But I was then too busy wolfing "iron" rations—bully beef and hard biscuits—and gulping *char* to bother about much else. The charge was behind me. The need of the moment was to fill the inner man. An army marches on its stomach. How true! Feed the brute and he will remain as brutal as you wish him to be. I could actually feel happy in the knowledge that there was food around.

Somebody once referred to Mesopotamian Force "D" as "hastily raised and improvised soldiers." Correct. For the most part we were raw enough. Though we did not remain raw for very long! But it always amused me to hear the enemy's force referred to, rather contemptuously, as "irregulars." I believe a great many of them were troops sent to Iraq in disgrace. They had nothing to be ashamed of, however, in their attitude towards us.

To appreciate a campaign such as we had engaged upon, it should be understood that Mesopotamia is largely a flat expanse of sanded waste, with many miles of barrenness between the towns and the villages and the occasional date palm groves, and at that time the country was entirely without railways, the only means of transport being the camel and the donkey. We collected river craft at various stages of the advance, but these were inadequate either as support in action or transport for an advancing force.

The Indian Government, which was responsible for the campaign up to the fall of Kut, seemed unaware of the fact that an-ever-advancing army required an increasing body of transport to bring up rations, equipment and munitions. We just muddled on from day to day, not knowing how far our successful engagements would carry us. We went on without lines of communication. We went on to our doom.

But the mere Tommy went on in ignorance of his fate. How should he know that he was going further and further away from his base and that no adequate lines of communication were being built up behind him? He trusted the powers-that-be and obeyed orders.

We occupied the village of Meezra and sat down upon it and thought ourselves conquerors. We had hardly begun. That night Steve and I were among the bunch dragged out for patrol. It is the Tommy's privilege to grouse. So we groused. It mattered not that we had marched most of the day and had fought a tough engagement. Out we went, trudging round and about the cluster of hovels in the darkness. It was certainly an experience. Lights are unknown in the crooked lanes and byways of Arabian towns. Occasionally we would see a feeble glimmer through the cracks of a shuttered house.

The village was as silent as the grave. Our tramping feet echoed and re-echoed. A muffled howl came to us sometimes. It was the jackal pack on the prowl. We had to do our three hours. In that thick blackness and mysterious silence it felt like three years. Once our sergeant darted forward into the blackness and grabbed at a slinking figure.

None of us had much Arabic on our tongues in those early days, but we gathered that the prowling Arab was protesting his innocence before Allah. He was unfortunate. We had our orders. The natives of the village had had theirs. They were not to move out of their homes after dusk. So the poor devil was booted along until he came to the house he indicated as his own. The N.C.O. went inside with the Arab—for what reason I have never been able to discover. Maybe it was just curiosity.

Anyway, the patrol remained outside and waited for the sergeant to come forth again. We kept on waiting. We grew uneasy. Somebody suggested that maybe the household was treating the sergeant to a mug of *arrack*—the liquor of Iraq that is distilled from dates and is very potent. We heard a shout. The voice was undoubtedly that of our

N.C.O. A deadly silence followed. Then we broke ranks and dashed towards the house. We crashed the gate and into a courtyard.

"Wait!" yelled Steve, as we reached the black cavity of an open doorway. He took out a flash lamp and played it about the interior. We entered cautiously behind him. He seemed to have taken charge of the twelve of us.

The room looked empty. It should be appreciated that we were in a strange village, in a land of which we knew nothing, and among a people whom we knew to be utterly treacherous. To us Tommies, they were "dirty Arabs" from the word "go!" And there was not a sound in that queer abode.

Then somebody gave a shout. We found the sergeant huddled up in a corner. He looked a bit green about the gills, but he was quite aware of our presence.

"A couple of you fellows had better get me back to the lines as quickly as possible. Jump to it, now."

"What's happened, sarge?"

"I walked in here with that Arab. He called to his women. Three of 'em appeared. Before I knew what was up, one of 'em suddenly lifted her foot and gave me a sickening wallop. I shouted and dropped like a log. . . ."

That sergeant was a decent fellow and a favourite among the men. Our feelings can be imagined. Two of the boys picked up the N.C.O. and carried him off back to the lines. The rest of us started to search the house. It was a weird job. There was something sinister about that dark and silent abode. We went from room to room, aided only by the indifferent light of a torch. . . .

"Blimey!" said a little cockney, "if I could lay me 'ands on that jane. . . ."

He expressed the feelings of ten weary and infuriated men. This incident has no military significance. Those who look for such had better stop reading now. If my tale has purpose it is that parents of boys still in their teens should know that war is not altogether a question of fighting. These are the kind of "adventures" that Tiger encountered. They are the inevitable issues of war. They play the devil with a boy's moral growth.

The episode had its sequel. The more those men searched, the more sick and weary and maddened they became. By the time they had ferreted out the women they were hardly human. Certainly they did not act like human beings. Half a dozen of them fell upon three women. I could only look on in horror. I noticed that Steve took no part, and I loved him all the more for standing out. He may have been a tough, hard-case *wallah*, but he usually managed to keep a cool head.

The piteous cries of those women ring in my ears now.

I don't know to this day what it was all about. I can guess that those women thought the sergeant was alone when he entered with the Arab, and somehow mistook the purpose of his visit. I do know that the N.C.O. sustained a serious injury and was sent down the line.

A detachment of men came up at the double. The ten of us were placed under arrest. When we stood before the C.O. he gave us a lecture on taking the law into our own hands—and left it at that. After all, he could not be bothered with such trifles. There was a war on.

And then the flood. We made a flanking movement towards the Tigris. There was a naval party moving up stream, but when we joined the main force we found that the army must get afloat as well. The river had overflowed its banks for miles, extending as far as the eye could reach. Here and there were oases of palms in little groups and belts. The flat-roofed, mud-brick native villages on higher ground stood out like little islands in a great ocean.

Obviously we could only advance in boats. The transport had to make wide detours, which resulted in disaster and delay. The Turks had their artillery in position on a range of sand hills rising out of the flood, and their advantage can be well imagined. To us Tommies, it looked like an impossible task.

There were two brigades in that action. We used all sorts of river craft, including about three hundred *bellums*—long graceful native boats that could be poled or rowed, and most of these were armoured by using machine-gun shields fixed on the bows. It was impossible to define the Tigris banks in that area, so great was the flood. Then, just to make matters more exciting, one of our armoured tugboats discovered a number of mines a few miles beyond Kurna.

We had to cross the flood to the eastern bank of the Tigris and beat the enemy out of their entrenched positions. The sand eminences on which the Turks had set their field guns were named Norfolk Hill, Two Gun Hill, One Tower Hill and the like. In that advance, our naval unit kept up a terrific gunfire on these hills while the troops laboured with the *bellums*, pushing, punting, rowing, struggling with the thick weeds in—which Arab irregulars were hidden—scrambling through deep-water currents, working and fighting like galley slaves in order to close up with the enemy's redoubts, which, all the while, were pouring out shrapnel in deadly showers.

This was Townshend's first task after landing in Iraq. It seemed that from the moment the general entered the country he was in the midst of the most extraordinary battles. Not only had we the appalling results of the flood season to contend with—but the hot season too. Scores of fellows flopped out of those *bellums* with heat stroke and were never seen again. Men were knocked out with shot and shell. And what chance has a wounded man when precipitated into weed-strewn waters far beyond his depth? Many a poor devil was shot first and drowned afterwards. The rest of us had to keep going. We dared not stop to help the wounded struggling for their lives in the weed-entangling water. It was our job to cross. . . .

Throughout it all our gunboats kept up a devastating fire on the hills. . . . I shall not soon forget the moment when the boats of our group grounded at the foot of one of those hills. The action was so much a repetition of our original landing in the country! We scrambled out of the boats and raced across the sand towards the Turkish redoubts. Shells were screaming over our heads—both ways. A young infantry captain who was leading us suddenly crumpled up. He died instantly.

The guns ceased. A white flag appeared. We found the redoubt knocked to pieces. There were two Krupp field guns as prizes—and a wounded Turkish officer. The rest had fled. Not until then did we have an opportunity to look round on the battlefield under water. It presented the most amazing scene. Timbers, rafts, shattered boats, dead bodies, pieces of equipment—the rag-tag of battle floating around everywhere.

The sun blazed down on it all. The heat haze was blinding. Steam rose from the patches of wood. Dirty, sweating Tommies dropped in their tracks exhausted. But we were on dry land.

Troops were coming up in all directions, scrambling over the range of sandhills like so many flies. Except for an occasional *phut-phut* in the distance, firing had ceased. The brigade was massing into something like formation, or at all events, that's what it looked like to me.

"Guess there's more trouble ahead," commented Steve, shortly.

There was. This was only the first phase. The order went round that we were to continue the attack at daybreak the next day on the main position at Bahran. Meantime we went around in fear of mines and bombs. If we saw an old can, a bottle, even a boot, we stepped gingerly round it. The Turks had a habit of leaving these things along the line of retreat!

The enemy was quiet that night. We made hip-rests in the sand—until an appalling stench told us we were a trifle too near a trench full of Turkish corpses. We moved on. It takes a lot to keep a tired Tommy awake. I slept like a log, in spite of the conditions.

We advanced on Bahran next morning. Sloops and gunboats were demonstrating from the river. All the way up from Kurna to Amarah the villages and towns were displaying white flags, Arabs, men, women and children, were running out of the houses to greet us, *salaaming* and *kow-towing* for all they were worth. If those natives could have understood the gutter English that was bawled at them, they would not have looked so pleased. Only a day or two before, these Arabs had been very much on the side of the Turks and fighting against us. Tommy's opinion, voiced in no uncertain terms, could hardly be written here.

Taking Amarah was like taking a baby's comforter. It was too easy. When we steamed up the river and came within sight of the town—it runs down to the water's edge—it was already ours. Three men had taken it! General Townshend had sailed up the river after the Turkish gunboats, some of which were shelled and crew and troops taken prisoners. At Kila Salih, the *khan* of the town went aboard the British sloop. He was told by the general to collect supplies for 15,000 troops who were coming along, for which he would be paid.

That was the ruse which gave us Amarah without a single shot being fired. As General Townshend had anticipated, the Arab chief sent the news to the Turks at Amarah. The result was that when the British gunboats reached the town—many hours in advance of the troops—the Turks were ready to surrender. A lieutenant, the coxswain of the boat, and a Tommy, went ashore; and these three received the surrender of the Turkish battalion and marched them down to the water's edge, where they were taken aboard an iron lighter. The general then had the lighter anchored in midstream and under the guns of his sloop! In the general's own words:

It must be remembered that I had only about twenty-five British sailors *and* soldiers with me.

The enemy, however, had been made to believe that a fleet of ships and 15,000 British troops were on the general's heels, when, as a matter of fact, he was two or three days in getting his force assembled around Amarah!

Amarah is a town of considerable importance with about ten thousand inhabitants, from which caravan routes lead to Kut and the Persian passes. It is some seventy-five miles up the river from Basrah.

The advance from Kurna to Amarah was a splendid piece of work on the part of General Townshend, but we had no idea then how far we were to advance up this strange country. It seemed that we were just wandering on and on, taking all we could. We had long ago passed the oil wells area, for which this Mesopotamian campaign was originally planned. Already there was talk of pushing further on as far as Kut-el-Amarah, more commonly known as Kut. There were even rumours that we might attempt the task of driving the Turks from Baghdad—which is 500 miles by the Tigris route from Basrah!

The unusual conditions of the country, however, forbade any further advance for the time being. It was the month of June, and the heat blazed down on Amarah with the breath of a giant furnace. The temperature registered as much as 125 in the shade. It was too much for the troops, most of whom had never experienced anything of the kind. Hundreds of them were dropping down with heat stroke, malaria, dysentery, and the flat-bottomed river steamers were crowded with sick moving down to Basrah.

Then Townshend himself went under with the heat and was sent down stream to take ship for India. We knew then that there was not likely to be any more scrapping until the cool season came round in September. In short, there are seasons in Iraq when it is too hot to carry on a war!

Thus we had two months of fatigues and other forms of idleness in the historic town of Amarah. It was then that young Tiger learned what all inexperienced youngsters with an army at war must learn—that an idle soldier's thoughts have but one direction, liquor and women.

During the first few days of our stay at Amarah the Arabs were inclined to be hostile, for they had learned how cheaply we had taken their town from the Turks. Various orders were issued. No soldier must patrol the streets alone. It was inadvisable for any but double-armed guards and police patrols to be absent from quarters after dusk. But you cannot make a fighting adventurer out of a civilian and then expect him to behave like a normal human being.

In my eyes it was all very adventurous and romantic and picturesque. Steve and I trailed around the bazaar quarters for days on end, acquiring a smattering of native *patois*, getting acquainted with the strange ways and customs of these dirty but somewhat fascinating brown people.

We used Indian *rupees* for money—and money talks. There were all manner of thrills and excitements in the *bazaar*. For the time being, the ugliness of war was forgotten. We made contact with the natives. We began to use their wine shops, their *cafés* and questionable amusement dives. We went into forbidden places—with a wary eye on the redcap, the military policeman; but that possible risk merely spiced the adventures.

It was cool in the shade of the *bazaar*. In the beginning one was nauseated by the stench spices, garlic, rancid butter, putrid mutton black with flies, tiny, smoky fires of dried camel dung, dust and decay, sweating eastern crowds, an effluvium that shocked the senses. Then one grew accustomed to it, even became captivated, felt drawn towards these strange sights and sounds and smells.

I can still smell those hot afternoons, still visualise the thoroughfares crowded with a jostling jumble of Arabians, Assyrians, Armenians, Jews and Persians. They were trading and bartering as if there were no war hereabouts. Merchants had resumed their restful cross-legged pose, each squat in the middle of his wares, like a Buddha idol set in a heap of antiques.

Somewhere, somehow, they had unearthed a cartload of goods curios, ornaments in brass and bronze, caskets and cabinets in carved sandalwood, ancient pieces of musketry, jewelled swords and the ornamental curved knives of Mecca, *bric-à-brac* of every conceivable sort. No doubt most of it had been looted, for they were busy looting the houses the Turks had hurriedly evacuated when we hove in sight, and it was necessary to shell the place before we could walk in.

In a few days they had settled to their more or less peaceful pursuits. Once more the cries of vendors and merchants rent the air. It seemed as if the little narrow streets, walled on either side by dilapidated buildings, would burst under the pressure of the pulsating, multitudinous life pouring through them in opposite streams.

The Arabians have a curious, fatalistic mentality. Surely no other people in the world could have settled down so nonchalantly and so quickly under the government of a strange people. Yesterday the Turks were their master. Today the British. What did it matter? Life does not wait on masters.

At the doors of ramshackle shops and booths, dry-featured, long-bearded old *sheiks* sat drinking scented tea, chatting of domestic affairs, smoking the long Arabian cigarettes that stank of burning herbs. One wondered what they thought of our intrusion. Whatever they thought no one among them betrayed a sign. They looked placid and peaceful, even venerable. We knew they could be as treacherous as hell.

We found one dive particularly amusing. Steve christened it the Sink. The name was apt. I fancy it was fixed up in a hurry to attract the visiting troops. It became a rendezvous. Gallons of aniseed-flavoured *arrack* were sold there. It was gay and boisterous. Tired Tommies appreciated it. The first time I looked upon the scene, the roistering men, the giggling girls in their laps, the dancing, singing, rollicking mob, I found it hard to believe that only a few days before the brothers and fathers of these laughing girls were ranged on the side of the Turks in bloody war against us!

That seems to be an essential part of war—blood one minute, love the next. But, as a famous general once said to his lady love, I did not come here to talk of war but to enjoy myself. And the brown girls didn't care. Maybe they thought these English were fools to pay for their love. The Turk was in the habit of taking what he wanted.

After witnessing death by shot and shell and drowning, what were tired Tommies to do with their bit of leisure?

One night we sat around the Sink while a sun-kissed child in beads gave us a curious exhibition, half dance and half contortionist act. She could not have been more than fourteen years, but then that is full womanhood in the East. Certainly she knew all the tricks. She had a round baby face and a red blob of a mouth, but her black velvet eyes had the expression of someone very old and very wise. She was of shapely mould, soft and supple and as flexible as rubber. All of her whirling posturing, pirouetting tricks seemed to be designed to draw attention to the big green glass ornament that hung from her neck. The movements of the glittering thing fascinated one, drew one like a magnet, played on the sensory nerves, until one's mind whirled in unison with the bewitching child.

I was raw then. Later I learned that such tricky exhibitions were common in these low eastern dens.

Of course, I tasted of the country's one and only drink—*arrack*. It is colourless, looks like water and as harmless, but it has a devil of a kick. Tiger, being a young fool who would try anything once, took more aboard than was good for him. And that upset everything.

I can dimly recall making overtures to that child-woman in beads. I must have been mad. I would have none of Steve's restraining hand.

"With your fair hair and blue eyes, Tiger, she'll eat you up!" roared Steve, who was also pretty well oiled.

That was something else I had to learn by experience—that my particular colouring was attractive to the easterner. Anyway, before I realised what was happening, I was standing up to a brawny Arab, prepared to fight for my own. He was big enough to break me over his knee, but I was filled with aniseed fumes and a torturing desire to hold that little devil in beads.

So, like a terrier after a wolf-hound, I flew at the brawny Arab. He didn't know much about fisticuffs or the art of wrestling. In no time I had the knuckles of both hands bleeding, dripping blood, but it was mostly Arab blood. Once he clutched and held me—like a big bear holding a cub. But I knew how to wriggle out of that. The boys were shouting and yelling encouragement. Some of the girls were scream-ing, some laughed in a fuddled sort of way. It was frightfully exciting, and I knew I just had to down that Arab by some trick or other.

"On the point of his jaw, Tiger! Go on! Shoot him one!"

Obviously I was trying to do that, but every time I got near enough his great arms shot out, clutched, and then started hugging the breath out of my body—until I'd sense enough to work the squirming, wrig-gling movement. Each time I did that, the fellow was left standing and groping, which made everybody laugh.

"Slippery as an eel, ain't you, kid!" bawled Cockney Joe.

How long this pantomime went on I cannot say. The Arab drew on his natural defence—the knife. That was fatal for him. The boys rose like one man and fell upon him. In a few seconds they were tearing the clothes from his back and the beard from his face. Truly a ghastly spectacle. It brought other natives on the scene. Thereafter a regular free-for-all scrap with screaming, dancing women on the fringe, claw-ing at this and that. I did not stay to participate, for I had seen out of the corner of my eye the little girl who had started all the trouble in the act of slipping through a doorway. I followed.

Fuddled Tiger thought he had earned his right-of-way.

When I got inside that room the girl turned round and spat like a tigress. But I had gone too far to stop. What with the *arrack* and the excitement—my blood was up. I reached out to take.

I fancy it would have ended with something worse than a torn face—if the patrol had not burst in at that moment. . . . After which an ignominious march back to quarters under escort. I passed the night in the cells, a heavy, drugged sort of slumber. I did not mind that. What did astonish me was the story put up by the patrol corporal when I was marched before the C.O.

I could only gasp. According to this corporal I was a thoroughly bad lot. I started all the trouble. In a drunken fury I had attacked a peaceful native. My stupid action had led to a drunken brawl in which fourteen British soldiers and eleven natives became involved. Not satisfied with having stirred up trouble in a quarter of the town that was still hostile to our forces, I had then chased a native girl. . . .

I wondered for a brief minute of whom this fantastic corporal could be speaking. Surely he was not referring to one Tiger—to me?

Shock number two.

I was being awarded a certain barbarous type of punishment used in the field of action.

"Yes!" I gasped.

"Take him away!"

I received a prod in the ribs from the aforementioned corporal.

"About turn! Quick march!"

This particular type of punishment has been abolished in the British Army. During the Great War the British Press said so repeatedly. Some such statement was made in the House of Commons. I can only think such announcements were put out in order to appease the mothers and wives of the British boys and men who had left their civilian jobs and gone to war. It certainly was not abolished on the Mesopotamian front. I ought to know!

CHAPTER 2

Heat and Strife Between Battles

That particular sort of punishment was about as great a piece of irony as anything could be during that astounding period of ironic lies—the Great War of 1914-1918. While politicians were indignantly declaring that such types of punishment could no longer be tolerated in the noble army of civilians turned soldiers, I was tasting that devilish punishment.

No man who has undergone such treatment is ever likely to forget. It involves the most excruciating torture. Tommies have told me that the same thing happened in Flanders. I was not there. I don't state it as a fact—though I am personally satisfied with the descriptions given me by the boys who were on the French front. But in Iraq, with the tropical sun blazing down upon the helpless victim, while his lips blacken and crack and his tongue hangs out, it becomes something more barbaric than even its sadistic originators ever dreamed!

I was lucky. I had a pal named Steve Barry. He hung around most of the time with a sponge that was wet and cool and marvellous in its soothing effects. He dared any of the guards to interfere. Being an American, he did not appear to have the same respect for British military discipline as his brothers-in-arms. Which was just as well for me!

I am not grousing. I was fully aware that I had committed a serious crime in military law. It was right, in military law, that I should be punished. I merely suggest that the punishment hardly fitted the crime. The whole point is that in spite of public indignation and political denial, the punishment was awarded and carried out to the letter, not merely on the Mesopotamian front, but on others. And the same sort of punishment, or something hideously like it, will be used in the next war, because, as the merest novice in psychology must realise, it will be necessary.

True, one was allowed forty-eight hours off duty to recover. At the end of that time my mental outlook had changed. I was growing fast. I was then ready for anything. I developed a philosophy of my own. It was not without bitterness and cynicism. These facts are necessary for a proper appreciation of all that follows.

Less than a week later Steve and I had found another and even more wretched dive. There was an Armenian girl there with a dead white face, oval and shadowy like a consumptive, and a body as slim as a reed. She was the type for my reactionary mood. I could even refer to her as death-warmed-up and still get some sort of kick out of the episode.

There was nothing more than a soldier's love in that, however. A frail passing craft. Besides, I was dying to beat up some "dirty Arab," just to show I could do it. The opportunity came in quite an unexpected manner. A company had been out on a reconnaissance north of Amarah. Only two-thirds of it returned. A hostile force composed largely of Arabian irregulars had driven our boys back almost on to the town. That, I understand, was what the enemy called a victory. Our company was sent out to clear up the mess. We actually welcomed the diversion.

We force-marched through most of the night and came to rest at dawn behind a sand ridge. It had been desert trekking through the long silent hours and when daylight came we saw the route had led us directly east. The river was no longer with us, a fact which made us hug our water bottles and hope for the best.

It was a memorable dawn we witnessed over the ridge of sand. Up till then life had shown me nothing quite like it. The first sign was a grey pencilling of light in the sky, and suddenly the eastern horizon burst open, splashed a wealth of colour over the heavens and the earth, as if the sun itself had exploded and sent its gold and crimson colours streaming and flowing over the whole universe. The grey sand turned blood-red before our eyes, a singularly dark shade of red which to my mind seemed somehow sinister. Later I thought how symbolic it was of that waking day.

Away on our right flank was a belt of palms and the sharply-defined outlines of a hamlet. That, we were told, was the area used to trap the company that had gone this way before us. We munched iron rations and drank sparingly of water while the light came up and the new day was born. We were to pay a visit to that huddle of habitations with the express purpose of teaching the lads of the village a lesson.

After all, they must learn that they could not do these things to the British and get away with 'em.

Steve's head lay in the sand within a few inches of my own. It was so close that I could see the grey dust thick in the creases of his leathery jowl. He turned towards me and lifted an eyebrow in that funny way he had while his grin spread from ear to ear.

"I ain't no prophet, Tiger, old fellah; but I guess there's going to be fun over there. Look!"

The light was coming up more clearly now. I looked in the direction of his pointing finger. Others were staring. An ugly growl rumbled along the ranks of prone men.

"When the boys get a close-up of those—"

Out there in the sand were many queer shapes, like bundles of sacking left carelessly about. We soon knew. Moving to the whistle of the company commander, we spread out in extended formation and advanced towards those strange objects lying in the sand. The captain, marching ahead, suddenly lifted his sword, shook it up and down. It was the signal to double, an action that looked strange in that weird light. Not that we required any second bidding. The whole company thudded along like one man, the officers racing ahead and the non-coms chugging behind.

I cannot escape the details of that dawn. They were seared into the mind. When we reached those queer shapes in the sand we pulled up abruptly. They were Tommies, stripped of everything in the way of clothing and equipment and literally hacked to bits. Most of them were dead, but there were one or two that still breathed, despite the unspeakable mutilations. They were given the merciful bullet.

It was then that the boys saw red.

"At the double!" snapped the captain.

We raced forward in the direction of that cluster of palms, a wild ungovernable mob, four platoons of soldiers red with the lust of vengeance, yelling and blaspheming enough to waken the dead.

On we went, stumbling over melon patches, through ploughed fields, splashing along a stream, until we came to the first of the farmsteads. Men grabbed at shovels and rakes and other implements. Heaven knows why. For every man carried his rifle and full rounds of ammunition. Perhaps it was just indicative of their crazy blood lust. Dogs raced out towards us, snapping and yapping. They were silenced with death blows. I recall the vague figure of an Arab farmer, his two or three sons and womenfolk, all dancing around and lifting their hands to heaven. The boys took them in their stride, laid them flat, passed on.

As we reached the outskirts of the village a sharp volley crackled over us, in no way checking the pace. We stumbled on, firing as we went. Arabs were sniping from the house-tops. Some of our men went down in the crazy rush. A bunch of irregulars had got into formation across our approach. The company commander yelled to us to take cover. But it seemed that nothing could stop that wild charge. Not even that deadly hail of lead. No military tactics here. Just a blind dash of maddened men.

We descended upon that band of irregulars and committed the most unholy slaughter. Never shall I forget that ferocious onslaught. We chased them in and out of the hovels, up one crooked street and down another, killing with shovels and rifle-butts, spattering the walls of houses and the dusty byways with blood until the little village became a veritable shambles. Vengeance indeed!

Most of the villagers had flown into the desert at our approach. In less than an hour it was a dead village in every sense of the word. There was a house-to-house search for arms. We collected nearly three hundred pieces, a number of long Arab rifles, but mostly German *mausers* and automatics, and several hundred rounds of ammunition. We commandeered mules and a wagon to carry the stuff away. Evidently we had burst upon a village used by the enemy for arming irregulars against us. There must therefore be many other such centres within a few miles of Amarah.

It was true that Johnny Turk had stopped playing at war because it was too hot to fight, but that did not mean he was inactive.

We buried our dead and then retraced our steps. "We kill 'em with shovels" was to become a catchphrase in the company. It followed us about for months—right along the memorable advance from Amarah through Ali Gharbi, Sheik Saad, Hannah, Sannaiyat, Kut, Ctesiphon, and back to a besieged Kut; for there are types of men, usually the best soldiers, who cannot refrain from swaggering even about a killing with shovels.

After that episode our company came to be known as the "Slaughtering Seventh." Most of the troops went a bit crazy in those abnormal conditions. The intense heat is apt to raise the temperature of a man's blood. The humidity, the flies, and mosquitoes, the grit-laden dust that rose in clouds wherever men moved, the monotonous diet of bully beef, biscuits and tea, brought all manner of inflamed irritations to white men—boils, rashes, prickly heat and the like. Within a fortnight of our occupation of Amarah, two thousand men were in hospital.

It became a common occurrence for a man suddenly to run amok. Strangely enough, the natives had a great respect for the fellow who went berserk. A madman was a sacred being in the eyes of Allah. They said that a sand beetle had entered his brain, when, as a matter of fact, the real trouble was the blazing heat, bad diet and *arrack*. And of all the sad cases in Amarah at that time, the saddest and the maddest seemed to be collected together in our company.

It was not surprising therefore that we should be marked down for all the toughest jobs. There was one occasion when we went up the river in a couple of gunboats, with the sort of expedition that is euphemistically termed a demonstration. Some of the villages had been giving trouble at night.

We broke away in late afternoon, and we must have presented a weird spectacle. The two craft were camouflaged to resemble the landscape—with sanded earth, trees, bushes and palms. They each carried 12-pounders concealed in palm leaves, while the men lay hidden among the imitation ridges and bushes of the moving landscape.

I doubt if there is another river quite like the Tigris. It is astonishingly tortuous, twisting and turning and even flowing back on its own track. No stream could have been more suitable for our purpose. At every angle and bend the craft were continually scraping the banks and cutting away huge slices of earth, so that there were times when we really became part of the landscape and our deception was complete.

The night was well advanced before the ships reached the first of the troublesome villages. The moon was high, huge, orange-coloured, shedding an eerie radiance over the silent scene of river and dusty plain. There was something both ghostly and grotesque in the way our camouflaged gunboats crawled along that serpentine stream. The engines were turning and that was all. They made but a subdued chug-chug. We crept along like thieves in the night.

Such thieves we were! We were come to blow a couple of villages to bits. The headmen had been warned that if their sporadic raids on our camps around Amarah did not cease their homes would be shelled, razed to the ground. They had ignored the warnings, had continued to raid our horse lines and ammunition dumps, and had finally sealed their fate by stabbing a sentry in the back and stripping him of clothing and equipment. Hence the demonstration by moonlight.

"A swell night for the job," commented Steve, as he lay snugly in a heap of sand.

"Wish we could go on all night like this—go on and on as far as Baghdad!"

"Guess we shall, Tiger, but not right now. They say Townshend is on his way back. There'll be real fighting again when he gets among us. You'll see your Baghdad, all right!"

"Gosh! It must be a wonderful city—mosaic domes and minarets, arts and architecture half as old as time. . . ."

"And lovely dames! Come all over artistic, ain't you, Tiger?"

"It must be this marvellous night. Did you ever see such colour, such a mysterious green light? You know, Steve, it makes me feel what a lot of rotters we are. This isn't a night for blood and lust and shooting people to hell. Could you imagine anything more incongruous, any scheme more diabolic?"

"Yeah, I get you. Looks like the edge o' beyond to me."

"The edge of things, surely? In this vast world of sand, with the stream trickling through—why do we have to snake through it with our camouflaged, death-dealing craft? The world has gone crazy, hasn't it? Why, just here, we might be alone in the world. It's so empty and peaceful. The desert is alluring, you know, under a moon like that. It casts a spell over one."

"And it can be cruel, too, old fellah, cruel as hell. . . . Never trekked over desert, have you, Tiger?"

"No, but I should like to."

"You think so! Say, Tiger, it's the devil's own trick. I've done it. I know. When you're going on for days with nothing but sand and sand and more blankety sand. . . . ."

I did not know then that Steve and I, and others, would one day be doing that very thing. . . .

I was concerned only with that desert as it was then, lying like a great sheet of silver-green water as far as the eye could reach. An unearthly radiance lay over all. Nothing disturbed that mystic night, except the half-muffled chug-chug of the ships' engines. One sought forgetfulness. It was heavenly to shut out, if only for a little while, the horrors of the past weeks—even though one knew in the vague recesses of the mind that more bestial work lay ahead. I know I lay there, among the make-believe of sand and bush, mile after mile, half-hypnotised by the glamour of the night, dreaming in an eerie en-chantment of things I could not tell to a soul, certainly not to this tough, matter-of-fact pal of mine.

There ought to have been sprites and faeries riding in tiny *gondolas* over that silver-green lake. . . . I was on the borderland of dreams, maybe; but I shall not forget that wonderful night, ever. It gave me a brief respite from the blood and beastliness of this thing called war. After all, I was merely a boy. I felt I had a right to my dreams. The desert can inspire as well as destroy. I was tired of fighting and it was in my heart to wish that the silvery night would never fade, that this moon-filled stillness would go on forever. Even the *blasé*, hard-bitten Steve was impressed.

There is that in the atmosphere of a moonlit desert which reaches deep down into one, touches depths unplumbed by any other experience in life. What seems rational and beautiful then will take on an unreal air in the crude light of day. No one could describe the feeling, the rapture of such an atmosphere. At such a moment there is a heightening of the senses on to unaccustomed planes. Thoughts are elevated to the sphere of dreams. . . . Sentimental. Yes. What a ghastly world this would be without sentiment.

And then I felt the first vague stirring of uneasiness. Realities were creeping in. Away over the rim of that tarnished silver a dim shadow appeared. It grew bigger, began to take shape, became the unmistakable outline of a desert village one of the habitations we meant ruthlessly, wantonly to destroy. If the villagers had not time to leave, so much the worse for them! They had been warned. The maw of British prestige must fall.

"Well, Tiger. There's our meat."

A bend of the stream brought the village into full view. We were slowing down. To me, it seemed incredible that we should do this thing. The distance now was a matter of yards. The village lay some three or four hundred yards from the water's edge. We drew on so as to give the following gunboat manoeuvring space. The hamlet lay still as death. This then was their contempt for our warnings. The huddle of houses and tiny, straggling streets were quite well defined in the light of that moon. A clear target indeed!

The silence of the night was suddenly shattered by the high-pitched scream of a 12-pounder shell, followed a few seconds later by a terrific explosion. No damage was done, however. The shell sailed right over the house-tops, to explode in the shadows beyond. It was the final warning.

The effect was electrical. That dead village sprang instantly to life.

Men, women and children poured out of the houses in all directions, shouting and screaming, gesticulating crazily, running like mad things through the crooked lanes and out towards the open desert. There was something comic as well as tragic about those figures racing through the streets. The moonlight gave the scene a theatrical aspect, as if one looked upon some giant grand *guignol* of the stage, where grotesquely-clothed ants careered hither and yon in the maddest confusion.

Youngsters stumbled and fell in their haste, were quickly snatched up and dragged along. One old woman pulled at an obstinate ass. An Arab drove his family along with the aid of a cudgel. Another turned for a second, raised his hands to heaven, and yelled the curses of Allah upon us. Women with babies ran fleet-footed as hares. A woman fell and was dragged several yards by the hair of her head. Naturally they were expecting another shell to explode over their heads at any moment.

We received the order to jump ashore and advance on the village. It was our job to rake the place from end to end and make certain that no human being remained. We covered the intervening yards in as many seconds. I fancy many of the boys welcomed that diversion. The house-to-house search was a great opportunity for free-and-easy looting by moonlight! The temptation was too great for many a soldier.

The hamlet was not altogether deserted. Steve and I came upon a woman in bed in one of the hovels. She was gasping in the birth throes. She lay half in the shadow and half in the light cast through the hole in the wall which served as doorway. In her struggles she had torn most of her clothes. She was pointing and making guttural noises. But we required no explanation of her presence there.

"What the hell now!" snapped Steve.

"Gosh! We can't leave the creature here! She'd be shelled to bits!"

"You said it all, Tiger. I ain't having this on my conscience. Come on, fellah! We'll carry her out. You take her legs. . . ."

We carried her out while she screamed and kicked and struggled, and generally set up an appalling hullabaloo. The noise attracted some of the boys. *Their* instant conclusion was that we were manhandling a woman—a sort of prize packet left behind in the wreck. An officer came rushing up.

"What the devil are you fellows doing?"

"Playing the Good Samaritan—or the damned fool! I don't know which!" snorted Steve.

The officer stared at the struggling woman. There was quite enough light for him to see what it was all about.

"Good God!" he gasped, and turned away. "Take her down to the bank of the river. She'll probably die on the way. . . . But she'll be out of range of the guns anyway. Fall in, two men! Give a hand here! Now get away to hell out of this!"

We went—four stumbling men and one woman. What a party it was! Somehow we got her down near the river bank and dumped her in the sand. Whether she lived or died we never knew. We were back on the gunboat a few minutes later and lined up for roll call. As soon as it was ascertained that all men had returned, the two craft opened fire on the village. It fell like a pack of cards. Soon we were steaming up the river again, leaving behind us a blazing bonfire to mark the spot where once a troublesome village had stood.

It was a night out in all conscience. We were hurrying along to our next job! Perhaps these villagers who had taken to the plains would in some way warn their compatriots in the next hamlet. There was no sign of life in the place when we drew up on the opposite bank about three miles further up stream. We went through the same procedure. A shell was sent screaming over the house-tops. But nothing happened. Its shrill scream and blasting explosion was enough to waken the dead.

We were sent ashore to investigate, and moved warily up the bank towards the silent hamlet. There was not a sign of life anywhere as we approached. What had these cunning natives left behind for us? The gunboats' searchlights were played about the buildings. A halt was called within a few yards of the place. We could then see the wires stretched from house to house and about a foot from the ground. Obviously those wires were connected to detonating charges. We had only to stumble against them and the company would have been blown skywards!

"Too bad," commented Steve, succinctly.

"About turn! Double!" bawled the captain.

"Run, legs, run!" laughed Cockney Joe.

And run we did. There is no describing our relief at that escape. We sped back to the ship like greased lightning. Then the guns began. This time they were dropped on to the buildings. For several minutes we enjoyed the spectacular firework display. When the shells hit those wires or the buildings to which they were attached, great showers of fire leapt skywards. It was a wonderful sight, a sort of Crystal Palace and Coney Island rolled into one. Detonators were popping in all directions and the shell-bursts threw bricks, timbers, household goods, showering into the heavens. Long after the shelling had ceased there were intermittent explosions from the charges.

The two gunboats were made fast. Our work was not yet done. The C.O. decided that the company would make a sortie at dawn. We could not allow these cunning *wallahs* to get away with a trick like this! Two hours to go, and in that time we got what sleep we could. There was not much rest for the Slaughtering Seventh.

Dawn came and we disembarked once more. There was little left of the village except burning debris. We opened out to extended order over the plains, and after marching for an hour found the ridges and sand dunes scattered about with shapeless bundles. Dead Arabs. The order went round that we were not to touch the huddled-up figures. It was not that we might have looted the bodies. We had grown to distrust the natives and knew that they would not stop at using their own dead to trap the living with hidden bombs. They were experts at bomb camouflage.

Just how those dead got there was a mystery—unless they had been blown from the village. Maybe this was the result of some tribal feud. There seemed to be hundreds of them lying around over a wide area. We passed on, still speculating on this queer phenomenon.

Then we had the shock of our lives. We were in a trap. The "dead" Arabs who had lain scattered about the plains suddenly rose, very much alive, and leapt upon us! In a few moments the whole company was thrown into the greatest confusion. Apparently the band, the same that had been responsible for setting the village with bomb traps, had seen us leave the gunboats, and since they must face us this was the crafty thing they had planned. Very neat.

Our captain was yelling at us to close in and rush the Arabs with bayonet charge. The sound of his voice certainly brought us to our senses. The majority of the band was between us and the river. We turned upon them. Our company, of four platoons, then numbered about two hundred, which put us on fairly equal terms with the natives. So we went to it. We were at close quarters in as tough a scrap as any soldier could wish for, and the Arab irregular is no child in a hand-to-hand scrimmage.

Our company commander had a deadly sword. He could decapitate as easily as another would slice cheese. And he did! Just the same, those Arabs went to work as if they were pretty certain of the outcome. They shouted, as sword and bayonet flashed and scraped, of *Allah* and the prophet Mahommed, fiendishly exulting in this opportunity to spill the blood of the *infidels*. Every battle is a religious one to the intrepid Moslem. *Allah* came to every scrap of theirs, and they just loved to say so while they fought, foaming at the mouth with leather-lunged shrieks and yells.

So we started bellowing and hallooing too—just to show maybe that we were not to be frightened by any vociferation about a favourite deity! Mad! But what would you in such ferocious and frenzied circumstances.

No man who has been in a bayonet charge, or a close-quarter battle, can ever tell exactly what happened. Such fighting has only one meaning—every man for himself and the devil take the hindmost. One is driven to an astonishing pitch of excitement, and to get through without a nasty jab is more a matter of pure luck than any skill in handling the weapon.

Our ranks were thinning terribly. One sensed that much. But the noise continued. The blaspheming did not abate. Blood-stained faces and blood-splashed clothes flashed across one's vision. We fought while the sweat poured. Men grunted like stuck pigs, died with curses on their tongues. Killing is a small matter among Moslem people who breed like rabbits. God! What a beastly scramble it all was! Never was there such a dawn. We were slashing right and left for an incredible period. Groaning men were trampled in the grey dust of the plains. And in the middle of it all, swinging a sword like one possessed, was the company commander. He flashed back and forth before one's blurred vision, the visor of his jaunty cap drawn down over an eye dripping blood. His the charmed life. He was, as far as one so heavily engaged could judge, having it all his own way.

Then came the sound of feet thudding over the dusty plains. One guessed what that must mean. The gunboat commanders had seen through their glasses what was happening to us, and at grave risk to themselves had stripped their ships of sailors and sent the detachment to our aid. The Arabs might well have given us a dreadful licking—if it had not been for those Jack Tars. They came up at the double with drawn swords and fell upon the encircling mob we had failed to break.

There followed a frightful quarter of an hour. The band, or what was left of them, broke away and raced across the desert. We followed. We had then tasted too deeply of this bloody combat to leave one man standing. That, in short, was how it closed. Each running figure was followed, caught, slaughtered. . . .

Thereafter a spot of fatigue, attending to wounded, burying the dead, for these latter were too many to carry down to the gunboats and back to Amarah. Nearly half the company went under in that crazy affair. The young captain had fought with only one eye to aid him most of the time. The two gunboats, apart from sending every available man, could do naught but stand by and watch. They dared not fire their guns for obvious reasons.

When we left the spot there were still many strange shapes scattered about the plains, but they were really dead then, not just shamming.

All this, be it noted, was but a sideline in the Mesopotamian campaign, for this was the "resting" period when the Turkish and the British forces found it too hot to continue the game of flying at each other's throats!

But then we were the Slaughtering Seventh. We had a reputation to preserve. Give a company of soldiers a name, good or bad, deserved or undeserved, and it will stick.

We went downstream to Amarah with all possible speed. We had accomplished that for which we had been sent out—but at what a cost! Enlistment in the British Army used to be called "taking the King's shilling." Tommy's interpretation of that was that men are cheap. They cost a bob apiece, while a horse might cost as much as fifty pounds sterling.

As soon as we got back to quarters the Slaughtering Seventh was made up to strength. It seemed to me that those in authority picked all the worst scoundrels they could find among the 12,000 or so then stationed around Amarah and shoved them into our company. There surely never was such a wild and ferocious mob. The men of the company became so truculent and obstreperous that it was necessary to keep them employed on some stunt or other. Every N.C.O. was an "old swat," that is, a regular army man of the toughest kind, and the officers were mainly mosquito-salted warriors from India.

It looked at times as if we were being detailed to police the whole desert. We were dedicated to hunting Arab bandits and stray detachments of irregulars that were forever causing trouble around the camps. Life for us was made up of expeditions over the plains to various strongholds of hostile natives—a perpetual guerrilla warfare that went on from day to day with sickening monotony. There was no respite.

38

Things came to such a pass that the men talked openly of desertion—though where in heaven's name they could go was a mystery to me. Nevertheless, the temper of the mob was definitely mutinous.

We returned to camp from a perfectly gruelling job one day, only to learn that we were detailed for fatigue—which took the form of building a road through one of the camps. This was too much for the boys of the Seventh. An ugly murmur ran through the ranks. It rose to an angry bellow. Officers and N.C.O.'s attempted to quell it by voicing threats of punishment. In a few minutes we were surrounded by detachments of other regiments. The rifles of our brothers-in-arms were levelled at us. In this way we were persuaded to take up the picks and shovels and go to the job.

We went. We bent our backs in the stifling heat and laboured at road-making—just like a gang of convicts. We were under open arrest. Guards, officers and non-commissioned officers patrolled up and down and kept a wary eye on these mutinous men of the Slaughtering Seventh. A group of natives had collected to watch the fun. They were tickled to death to watch these white men labouring like nigger slaves. Their sneers and jeers did not escape us. This was adding insult to injury with a vengeance. A wiser commandant would have had those natives driven off and sent about their business. . . .

"These guys just grouse, and leave it at that," was Steve's comment.

But he was wrong. There was that in the air which convinced me that further trouble was brewing. I could feel it in my bones. Suddenly about a score of men with shovels broke through the patrolling guard and dashed upon the grinning Arabs. The act was so totally unexpected that the natives had no chance to flee. They were surrounded by enraged and infuriated men. Spades and pickaxes whirled through the air and the Arabs went down like nine-pins.

In a few moments the whole camp was in an uproar. Shrill whistles rent the air. A detachment of armed men came up at the double. The boys with the shovels were dragged from the scene of slaughter and marched away under escort. That ended our fatigue for the day. The remainder of the company was dismissed.

Now, there is in the British Army a punishment known as pack-drill. The delinquent appears on parade in full marching-order equipment—belt, straps, ammunition pouches, knapsack, water-bottle, haversack, great coat, entrenching tools, rifle, bayonet and other trifles, all of which weigh about 25 lbs.

Owing to the intense heat in Mesopotamia much of this was discarded, and the troops marched without tunics. The Tommy awarded packdrill, however, wore the whole collection. Thus heavily burdened, he was ordered to march up and down in a given area, while an N.C.O. would stand by and bawl repeatedly: "About turn! About turn! About turn!" This caused the unfortunate one to swing at every few steps with his load of clothing and accoutrements, and the effect may well be imagined.

This was the punishment awarded the twenty men of our company who fell upon the jeering Arabs. Packdrill, they said in England, was not permitted in the Mesopotamian Campaign, as it was too severe a punishment for tropical climates!

CHAPTER 3

Battle of Kut

General Townshend was back in Amarah by the end of August, 1915, from his sick leave to India. Great preparations were being made for a planned advance on Kut, though at this time we were still registering temperatures of no to 117 in the shade! Our river transport had been increased, but the important land transport for an advance in such a country was very inadequate. The general recorded this at the time in a letter to Sir John Nixon:

> [1]I am afraid my advance will seem slow to you, but it cannot be avoided, when I have to battledore and shuttlecock my transport about to fetch up troops and stores in homoeopathic doses. . . .

The troops were being moved up the river in steamers and barges to Ali Gharbi. Apparently the main body of the fighting force was to be concentrated there. Barges were lashed port and starboard of a steamer with the dual purpose of protecting the vessel in the narrow, twisting stream and also to accommodate a greater number of troops. Our company was on a barge starboard of the steamer. We were continually scraping the banks, running so close, in fact, that we could easily have stepped ashore!

Perhaps the most striking feature of that memorable upriver trip was the utterly primitive state of the people who dwelt on the lonesome banks. Those marsh Arabs were conspicuously scanty as to clothing. The children just ran around in their birthday suits, wearing nothing but a smile, while their elders seemed to wrap themselves indifferently in bits of sacking.

---

1. *My Campaign in Mesopotamia*, by General Townshend, K.C.B., D.S.O.

We passed tiny farmsteads and ragged habitations. Natives in rags were tilling the land, working ancient water wheels with bullock power, fishing from broken-down jetties—yet they appeared picturesque in a rugged sort of way. At some points we scraped the river bank for miles, and there men, women and children ran alongside our barge to trade with us in eggs, chickens, fish, and any odd ornamental bits they happened to be wearing.

Some of them dropped into the water, awaited our coming, then, one hand on the barge rail, they waded the slushy water, looking about as attractive as scarecrows after a downpour. Trading with these primitive folk resolved itself into a game of chance. The method was to throw your *rupees* into the sack-cloth of the dirty but smiling women which single garment did duty as blouse, skirt and shop counter—and a small basket of eggs would be handed over the rail to you, if you were lucky!

One charming damsel, with a face like a dockside labourer, waded up to the rail where I was standing. One saw that though she was still young she was as hard and taut and as full of muscle as a prize-fighter. She slipped off her bangle, a bit of beaten bronze and the only ornament she possessed, and offered it for sale. I held up two *rupees* as a suggestion of the price—then equivalent to half a dollar. The hefty maid laughed her consent, and opened her mouth widely and invitingly. One at a time I threw the *rupees* into it. Deftly she caught each one. And then—she did precisely nothing! She remained standing, while the steamer continued its way upstream. She seemed to be shaking with mirth.

"Say, Tiger!" laughed Steve, "I guess you're the funniest thing that dame's seen in years! "

We reached Ali Gharbi, to find the place swarming with troops. All manner of activity was giving the area the appearance of an immense army at work. A vast expanse of the desert was covered with tents of all sizes and shapes—this, we later learned, was merely a stunt to give the enemy's intelligence the impression that the Mesopotamian Force was very much greater than it actually was. We totalled 11,000 combatants and about thirty guns.

It was from this centre that the real hardship began. We were force-marched through the desert for five nights, passing through villages and hamlets without firing a shot. Sheik Saad, Hannah and Sannaiyat we took in our stride. By September 15 (1915) we were massing at Abu Rummanah preparatory to the Battle of Kut—which was bigger

THE LADY WHO "SOLD TIGER A PUP!"

than anything we had so far encountered. We were then about eight miles from the Turkish lines.

The Turkish commander, Nur-ud-Din Pacha, had been concentrating his forces throughout the hot months, digging in hard and strengthening his position. He had settled in at Essinn, just below Kut, with three divisions, a mounted brigade and thirty-eight guns— 12,000 regular troops and 3,500 Arabs. At this point the Turks were sitting astride the Tigris with the fixed determination to keep the British out of Kut, since, once we had taken that town, there would be every likelihood of our continuing the advance *via* Ctesiphon to Baghdad.

Johnny Turk had therefore made an excellent job of his defences at Essinn in order to protect Kut. He was about eight miles from Kut, had entrenched himself on both sides of the river, and had a bridge of steamers chained together across the stream.

Though the British infantry units were in position for the attack by September 15, they had to remain idle for ten days while the river transport brought up the artillery and the howitzer battery. It was not until the night of the 25th that the last of these ships arrived. Such was the state of our transport facilities even after months of preparation. We know now that this state of affairs was due entirely to the niggardly attitude of the Indian Government, which was at that time controlling the campaign. General Townshend had begged in vain.

On the eve of this historic battle General Townshend published the following *communiqué* to the troops:

"The Secretary of State has telegraphed to General Sir John Nixon (Commander-in-Chief in Mesopotamia), wishing the 6th Division a speedy and complete success, to crown all their previous efforts, and to assure them that their services are not forgotten.

"In conveying this message to the troops, Major-General Townshend wishes to say that the Division has fought five engagements in the last eleven months, and has gained in the Empire a reputation second to none, be it on the banks of the Yser in Flanders or on the banks of the Tigris or Euphrates in Mesopotamia.

"There is no need for him to remind the troops of what their King and Country expect of them, and he hopes that a good blow now may well end their Mesopotamian labours."

By a bold and brilliant piece of strategy, General Townshend defeated the Turks at Essinn and advanced on Kut. Briefly, he rolled up the Turkish left flank after leading them to expect the attack on their right. On September 27 the feint was made on the right bank, a bridge was built, the crossing from right to left bank and the deployment of the infantry opposite the enemy's left flank were silently carried out during the night, and the enemy was taken completely by surprise.

Such are the historical facts of that battle. It is always interesting to the soldier who played his little part to learn afterwards just how it was done, for he himself can have no definite idea while the thing is actually taking place. He moves like an automaton. He does as he is told. He is there merely to obey commands. As Tommy would say— "Orders is orders."

My recollections of the affair are a little more hectic. I know that our company was part of a massed body that marched mile upon mile through that grim and silent night. The order had gone forth that no man must speak throughout the march, nor fuss with his equipment, nor do anything likely to create the slightest sound. It seemed to me that we were marching many miles into the desert—away from the river we had crossed—and that we were actually retreating!

We plodded on hour after hour, like a great ghost army, crunching the sand with phantom feet. Orders would come along, whispered from mouth to mouth, so that we changed direction like men on a drill square. One had the eerie impression there being nothing to do but march and think—that the ghostly hand of some all-powerful deity was moving us hither and yon as a man moves pawns on a board.

Anon the platoon commander would turn and whisper halt. The platoon would drop in its tracks, like a row of cards, silently. But there was no "cigarette space." Any sort of light was strictly forbidden. In a few moments we were up again crunch, crunch, crunch. It was the creepiest experience, moving on and on, to heaven knew where or what.

Dull, thudding feet. The monotonous thud-crunch was beaten into our ears. We must have presented a weird spectacle, a giant but ghostly shape looming through the glowering darkness of the night, a grim and sullen thing on a grisly and gloomy mission. No singing, no talking, no smoking—only the monotonous crunch of feet leaping in and out of the sand.

God! How one must fight to stop oneself thinking during the long and ghastly hours!

Though our feet were in step, it seemed to me that bodies swayed drunkenly in the dim column ahead, like stalks of wheat in the wind. And some wag of a fellow would whisper in a hollow sepulchral voice:

"How long, O Lord, how long!"

Afterwards we knew, of course, that that long night march was not a retreat, but a great, wide, sweeping manoeuvre on the enemy's left flank *and rear*. That is to say, we were working round the left of him in order to get behind his trenches before we struck. We were told that there were about eight miles between Johnny Turk and ourselves when we massed together for the big attack. I'll swear we marched twenty miles that night. A wide enough turning movement, in all conscience!

Dawn came and still we marched. So far as we could see, we were merely marching across the desert, since there was nothing to see but sand and sand, fold upon fold of wretched sand.

"Blimey!" quoth Cockney Joe, "we're lost!"

At the time we were doing it, it certainly seemed a purposeless thing to do. Nobody ever tells a soldier anything. So we were inclined to ask ourselves why on earth we were being dragged across the desert in this aimless fashion!

Then the rumour went along the ranks that we were taking Johnny Turk by the back door. We were advancing on his rear! The British Army lives on rumours. Nevertheless, as the sun came up we realised that this was one of the rumours that must come true. There was the great golden ball rising on our left flank. We were then marching south. It was an extraordinary experience, to march out of the night into the dawn and realise we were trekking down country instead of up country, as we had been doing for nearly a year!

But with that tell-tale sun rising to greater and greater heat, there was no mistaking the direction. Soon the strange outline of things came over the horizon. We began to pick them out. As we drew nearer they took more definite shape. We saw in the distance the earthworks, the dumps and stations that mark unmistakably a fighting force's rear lines.

No sooner had we got into view than a terrific burst of firing broke out, shattering the morning stillness. But it was not directed against us! Johnny Turk was defending himself against a frontal attack. It was then that we fully realised what this night manoeuvre to the rear of the enemy's lines really meant. But surely something had gone wrong? Could it be that the section of our force which had advanced for the *frontal* attack had so exposed itself that there was no option but to go into action? Looking back on it now, I know that such must have been the case.

At all events, we were suddenly wakened up out of our listless marching. The order went forth to prepare for action. Apparently we were late for the rendezvous. It mattered not that we had marched all night when the order to "double" came. Double we did, at that steady, military jog-trot that keeps men going indefinitely.

Then we saw the cavalry gallop into action. It was a cheering sight. They seemed to spring out of nowhere, out of the heat haze on both flanks, close in, and race hell for leather towards Johnny's back door. And we ran behind them, deployed into action. At the command of one man the whole desert had come alive. Men laughed and shouted, exhilarated by this sudden springing to life, relieved beyond measure by the action that broke the dead monotony of a night's marching.

When you tap that well of feeling in man which is called "boyish adventure," you tap more than you know. Streams of excitement and passion and blood-lust are brought bubbling to life. And who shall say at what point these may be dammed?

We went to that job of slaughtering the Turk in the manner of a lot of boys suddenly let loose in the playing fields. To us it was just an exciting adventure after the dread monotony of the hours that had gone before. Damnable as it undoubtedly is, there is a thrill about such a charge. Maybe it is that the beast in man is never far from the surface. It needs no great inducement to make the thing raise his ugly head.

Miraculously the weariness was shed and we were thudding along towards those trenches with fixed bayonets as though refreshed after a night of sound sleep. The thrill of the action had lent us a spurious strength and vitality. We could not get to those trenches quickly enough. We had trapped the other fellow, and that was advantage enough. There is nothing like having the advantage to give a fellow confidence! Johnny Turk was far too busy replying to the frontal attack he had expected and prepared for, to appreciate what was happening behind him—that is, until we were right on top of him.

We swarmed into the communication trenches without meeting any opposition. There was nothing to stop us at that point except the usual motley of cooks, stretcher bearers, officers' servants and such odd men generally to be found behind a fighting line. These we took in our stride. Getting in at the back door like this was no end of a lark!

It was then that we saw how busy the enemy had been during the hot "idle" months. He had built up a wonderful system of trenches, and had every justification for believing that the Britishers would not be able to oust him. He had reckoned without our back-door manoeuvre. The communication ways led us through wing trenches, third and second line trenches up to the main fire trenches.

To appreciate fully what that fighting below ground was really like, one should have some idea of a trench. Not everyone has seen a trench. Briefly, it is an elongated grave (how true!), deep and narrow, so that two men could hardly pass each other in the confined space. The communications were at right angles with the front line trenches, and from one to the other were turnings and angles leading to rests and dugouts. All along the subterranean passes we were jumping upon surprised men, the bayonet would strike once, and we would pass on. The trapped men, busy defending themselves against the frontal attack, had hardly a chance to turn to those who were paying a morning call by way of the rear entrance.

The result was those trenches became a veritable slaughter-house. Our sudden appearance brought the greatest confusion to the hapless men unable to face both ways. The dugouts behind the main fire trenches were raked with the bayonet. Men dropped their arms and threw up their hands, thinking naturally that we had come over the top from the frontal attack, and that being so, the show was all over.

Here was the element of surprise with a vengeance! I cannot forget how extraordinarily thrilling it was suddenly to turn a bend in the trench and come face to face with an astonished Turk! I never saw so much surprise revealed in the faces of men as during the hectic hours of that memorable morning. One after another we came upon them, all registering that rather silly look of amazement. It is so easy to down a man when he is taken by surprise.

Nor was the manoeuvre without its element of humour. I came upon Cockney Joe, that undersized little devil all wire and thong, at the door of a dugout, busily cutting the buttons off a Turk's trousers! Already he had four prisoners standing in a line, each one holding his waistband to prevent his trousers falling down! And he was at work on a fifth. There were more Turks inside that dugout but the little Cockney—himself hardly more than half the size of the men he was taking prisoners!—would only allow one man to come forth at a time, for he held a hand grenade and he was quite prepared to throw it in the dugout should the Turks fail to understand him. He knew that so long as his prisoners' hands were occupied holding up their trousers they were helpless. He told us later that by such means he managed to capture a score of men single-handed. It is probable that he exaggerated. He had a tendency that way.

We reached the front-line trenches to find that the fire of our own force was still coming over. In such an expediency there was only one thing to do. We had to silence these Turks who were busily replying to the fire of our brothers-in-arms out there, lest we receive some of the fire ourselves! To be shot by our own men was hardly the thing we had bargained for. I fear that in the desperate circumstances we went to it with unusual ferocity. The majority of the Turks were standing on the fire-step, their backs to us, heads down on the rifle butts, pressing the clips and firing as fast as they could go.

They were stuck in the back and pitch-forked unmercifully to the floor of the trench, for all the world as if one were stabbing sausages and dropping them into a can! Thus we passed along the frontline trench, sticking and dropping these unwary men, trampling them under foot in a frightful scramble of blood lust and sickening death. In that shambles the yelps and grunts and squeals, the cries of pain and the curses of *Allah*, made an appalling chorus for the crackling fire. True, as we progressed, those on the fire-step ahead were made aware of our presence. Many swung their rifles round and fired into their own trenches.

The raid went on for hours, scrambling up one trench and down another, and it was difficult at times to avoid clashes with our own men. Presently we realised that the fire was dying down. We rounded up the prisoners, collected our dead and wounded—a surprising number! Then a concerted thudding of feet, and we knew what it felt like to have a body of men charge and bombard one's trenches. They, however, had been warned of our presence. We joined forces and set to work to clear the entrenchments.

The Turks, we learned, had been working on this entrenching system since June. They had made elaborate use of plates, sleepers, timbers and other railway material that had been specially brought down from Baghdad to strengthen the field fortifications. And after all their work, a simple trick of military strategy had beaten them.

We had no means of knowing at that time what had happened on the front as a whole, since our responsibility was the left flank situated six miles from the Tigris. We knew vaguely that the river had been blocked by the Turks and that the enemy had a strong force on the right flank—where they had expected to fight the big battle. Nor did we care. By noon of that memorable day most of us were exhausted. We had marched all night, made a charge and stormed the trenches during the morning, so that it was not surprising to find men dropping down with sheer weariness. Added to which was the problem of water. The heat was blazing down and we were too far from the river. There was a marsh some distance from the entrenchments, but the water was poisonously bad. Just the same, many of the men were in such a state that they would drink anything, however filthy. Finally the order went round that we might rest for a while. We sank down in those trenches that stank of blood and the unhygienic habits of Johnny Turk and slept the sleep of the exhausted.

It seemed that I had hardly closed my eyes when I was being booted to my feet again. We were going straight into action! The Turks had brought up their reserves from the right bank of the river and across their bridge of boats near Kut with the intention of restoring the battle on the left wing. We climbed out of these fortifications and went to meet them. That was at sunset and some twenty-four hours since we had started out on this ghastly job.

We met Johnny in the open and gave him all the lead he asked for. He was not keen on a fire-fight in the open, and less keen about our advance with fixed bayonets. He retreated. He drew us towards his artillery fire—and we didn't like that. We dug in, each man working feverishly with his entrenching tools to make a hole big enough to shield himself. It is somewhat surprising to find how quickly one can make a trench, piling the dug earth in front of oneself the while, in such circumstances! Men do astonishing things under the stress of fire!

Darkness descended. The scream of shells was dying down. We burrowed and burrowed like great moles, sank deeper into our holes. Johnny Turk turned off the fireworks, at least, so far as our bit of front was concerned. We could hear an intermittent *phut-phut* in the distance, but evidently not meant for us. So we sank down and dozed while nursing the rifle-butt.

Steve, who had used a gun in all sorts of odd spots while I was still at school, was of the opinion that the battle of Kut was over. He argued that Johnny Turk would have driven us back and back in order to regain his trenches, if he had been strong enough to do so. He was right. When daylight came we were given the cheering news that Johnny had abandoned his defences and had passed on under cover of darkness.

As to the obstruction across the Tigris—thereby hangs a tale of wonderful determination and courage on the part of Lieut.-Commander Cookson, who was in charge of our naval unit. It should be noted that the river at this point had a navigable channel only half the width of the stream at Basrah, and that the trenches on both sides reached the river banks. The commander went forward with his three gunboats at dusk under tremendous fire. The obstruction was found to be a flying bridge made by an iron lighter running on chains.

The commander left his ship in a small boat, axe in hand, paying no heed to the terrific fire blazing all around him, an enfilade that riddled his ships and the little boat in which he worked. He was shot dead while in the act of severing the cable.

We captured 1,158 prisoners and fourteen guns in the Battle of Kut. Altogether the Turks lost 1,700 killed and wounded, and our casualties amounted to 1,229 killed and wounded.

General Townshend became the hero of the hour, and deservedly so. The men swore by him. Their confidence in him was nothing short of amazing. Even the Turks began to think him irresistible. The attitude of our prisoners was one of reverence This great general had achieved the impossible. He had routed the enemy from fortifications they had been building for months! Thus far, his troops had never been beaten. They had taken everything before them—thanks to his splendid generalship. But no thanks were due to the Indian Government for its niggardly attitude in the matter of adequate divisions, munitions, transport and general supplies. . . . This attitude was yet to prove the downfall of Townshend and his gallant troops.

In his story of the campaign, General Townshend wrote:

The battle of Kut-el-Amarah can be said to have been one of the most important in the history of the British Army in India. There had been nothing of its magnitude either in the Afghan war or the Indian Mutiny, for it was fought against troops well armed and of equal numbers to ourselves. In addition we ejected them from a very strong and up-to-date position commanding ground as flat and as open as a billiard table with nothing to check their fire-sweep.

CHAPTER 4

Love and Latifah

It appeared there was to be an interlude after the Battle of Kut. The powers-that-be were busy making up their minds as to whether we should stay put or advance on Ctesiphon which was the real protection for Baghdad. That advance did, of course, take place, on November 22, nearly two months after Kut. Meanwhile there was Kut and days of respite for tired Tommies. October brought some cessation from the intense heat, though it was still very much hotter than the hottest of summers at home, and the hospitals were full of sick and wounded.

At that time the town of Kut was an important centre, a sort of Mecca for the Arabian farmers, and there was considerable grain traffic in the neighbourhood.

We were to know Kut tragically well, to hate its every brick and stone—but that time was not yet. In the days immediately following our occupation we went about the highways and byways like the conquerors we were, confident and full of traditional swagger. We made full use of the town then, became familiar with its intricate alleys and strange quarters.

It was this very fact that nobody knew what was to happen next—Townshend was strongly opposed to any advance unless his force could be strengthened—which resulted in a somewhat lively episode on the outskirts of the straggling desert town—an affair in which I, all unwittingly, played an important part.

Cockney Joe, Steve Barry and I were pals together at this time. We made a habit of exploring every mysterious hole and cranny of the place. Eventually our wanderings led us to a secret dive beyond the town which offered more than the usual thrills and excitements. For one thing, the den was not frequented by the troops. It was a rendezvous for as rascally a mob of natives as one could hope to meet—which made it all the more interesting to us.

The native *habitués* should have strongly objected to the presence of three soldiers in their midst, but they did not. This might have been a suspicious circumstance to any but carefree, heedless, swaggering Tommies. The fact that we were the only white men there made the visits seem all the more adventurous.

Even when we became friendly with the young ladies no brown gentleman raised an eyelid. The liquor was the usual aniseed-flavoured *arrack*, for which, by this time, we had acquired something of a taste. The girls, however, were a vast improvement on the liquor. There were about half a dozen of them, uncommonly attractive, of the Armenian, Assyrian and Circassian persuasion—that is, all Christians in a den of Arabian Moslems, the pretty heritage left to the country by Turkish domination.

After a few visits we were on more than familiar terms with those girls. Perhaps the fact that they were of the West, not the East, gave them an especial appeal in our eyes. In that setting of sensual mystery and sordid intrigue those pale faces held an allure that was undeniable. Besides, there certainly was some mystery about the place. There were strange comings and goings. One's too-imaginative mind pictured it as the stronghold of some hostile band of natives. It turned out to be something much more sinister than that. . . .

The saloon itself went underground, was without any attempt at ornamentation. It boasted only a number of tables, crude wooden benches such as may be seen in any *bazaar* coffee shop, and a few flock-exuding settees. The floor was of beaten earth and covered with native mats. But it was the mysterious passages which led from this room that intrigued one.

I came to know one of those passages quite well. So did my two friends. There were rooms leading off it to which one could retire.

Boy as I was, I thought then that I had no delusions about women. But Latifah was different. She was a fascinating baggage. Hers was the true Circassian pallor, pure as alabaster, with that dull bloom so distinctive of the people of Mount Caucasus. She was small and dainty, with delicately poised head a dark cloud of hair and purple-black eyes, immense, unfathomable eyes. She had the baby mannerisms of her kind, was as soft and playful as a child.

And what more could a soldier want? In the beginning I hardly noticed her childish quizzing and questioning. I was too absorbed. But

A street in the Bazaar Quarter of Kut-El-Amara

with the passing of the days, the growing familiarity, and the fading of amorous attraction, I began to take a more intelligent interest in her, and in what I had thought were her childish queries in myself and my job as a British soldier. This soft and scented thing that had been able to rouse desire, now became a dangerous and sinister child. Not that her manner changed at all. Her calculating ardour never waned. She was too well schooled for any such error.

It was merely that my eyes had opened to this, for me, unusual situation. The childish queries persisted. I had to realise that I was a likely source of information. I was forced to conclude that all this, the acceptance of my two friends and myself in this secret den beyond the confines of the town, our apparent welcome in this strange gathering, had a definite and serious purpose.

But why pick on me? What could I, a common Tommy, know of our military movements and intentions? I tried to put the suspicion aside as something too utterly fantastic. But the evidence was too much for me. This child-woman, with her baby ways, had a serious intent that rather frightened me. I did not tell either of my friends about my suspicions. They would merely have laughed at me for a romantic young fool. I hate being laughed at. But I thought and pondered about the affair for days.

Not by word or deed—or lack of deeds!—did I show that there was any awareness on my part. I kept up the game, played it for all I was worth. Indeed, it was an enthralling game. I am not suggesting that I was unmindful of the risk attaching such a pastime. That made it all the more alluring. I know of no more fascinating pursuit.

This joyous baggage, even while she made love, would express her fear of losing me. *She hoped it would not be soon!* I was not to leave her yet, was I? Not for a long time? Would I not tell her and so ease her mind or words to that effect! In short, was the British force content with Kut, or was it planned to advance upon Ctesiphon and Baghdad? If so, when? To all my protests that I did not know what was to happen, that no one knew whether or not we should go further, she would complain that I was hurting her, that she loved me—*Je t'adore! Je t'adore!* in Baghdad French—and that she was terrified lest I should suddenly disappear one day without giving her any warning!

"You please me, desire of my eyes. Why should I leave you?"

"One day . . . you must."

"Who knows? Be happy now!"

"This day . . . when is it, *mon cheri?*"

"*Je ne sais pas.* No man knows."

"No man knows? *Le Capitan* ... he does not know?"

Then, in a flash, I saw why I had been chosen as a possible source of information. During our stay in Kut I had been detailed as batman to a certain officer in the political service! Evidently he was *le Capitan?* And I, his servant, would know as much as my master? But I never showed even by so much as the flicker of an eye that I knew what was afoot, now that Latifah had given herself away.

If she were not playing the game of decoy for some mysterious person behind the scenes, how came she to know about the captain? I had never mentioned him. I heartily disliked the job of batman. I had been in the habit of putting it completely out of my mind when on pleasure bent. Some fool of an intelligence merchant had thought to procure valuable information by way of the political officer's servant. Apparently my friends and I had walked into a hot-bed of intrigue and espionage of the native kind. It would be worth something to find out whether the British intended a further advance, or whether a date had been fixed for an attack on Ctesiphon, if we proposed to attempt Baghdad, and if so, what reinforcements we were expecting.

I was in Latifah's room when this thing was sprung upon me. If there was nothing of the Orient in the girl there certainly was in the room to which she was so fond of inviting me. Walls and floor were covered with Persian carpets. We seemed to spend our time lounging on a heap of gay cushions in the middle of the floor. There was a lamp that burned dimly, casting weird shadows. I was thankful for that dimness. It seemed to me, lounging there with the soft bundle nestling beside me, that I might draw the girl out, induce her to give more away. The conditions were as much in my favour as hers.

So that while we played the game of dalliance we indulged also in the pastime of a highly-spiced espionage and counter espionage. Just then, I felt no end of a smart fellow. If I could not outwit this soft, clinging thing. . . . Older men than I have fallen over the same sort of conceit! What I did not realise in time was that this girl was an expert in the art.

"*Le Capitan?*" queried I, innocently. "But he does not know."

"You have asked him, *mon cheri?*" she murmured, while soft hands caressed my face.

"No. I shall learn soon enough."

"Soon you will go?" she cried, mistaking my meaning.

"*Je ne sais pas!* No one knows."

"Je ne sais pas! Je ne sais pas!" she pouted. "You say you will learn soon! Then you say no man knows! It is that you know but will not tell me, *n'est ce pas?"*

"When I learn, it will be too soon, *comprez?"*

"Will you not ask *le Capitan?* So! Then Latifah will know!"

That was how I figured it, too! I left her that night with my head afire. I was as excited as the devil. I pondered deeply as we trudged back to quarters, wondering whether I should confide in Steve and Cockney Joe. There seemed no doubt about the little girl's game now. She was too persistent. I had the feeling that someone in the background was pressing her for the information she had so far failed to obtain. Were my friends being prevailed upon to talk! From their conversation it would hardly appear so.

"She's a regular hell cat, that Assyrian kid!" quoth Steve.

"Satani? Blimey, she's got the right sort o' name," agreed Cockney Joe.

The two were deep in a discussion on points. Apparently one thought his light-o'-love more of a spitfire than the other. And so on and so forth throughout the homeward trek. Neither appeared to notice that I was showing little interest. My mind had reeled away from such matters. It was chockfull of queries.

Could I talk to the captain when I went along to clean his kit in the morning? And what should I get for my pains? Maybe I should be told to leave the *arrack* and women alone, ordered to keep away from such dives. But I had gone too far. Young Tiger was in deadly earnest—stalking a spy! Events proved that I was right.

I decided before I fell asleep that night that I would confide in Steve. I would wait until the morning, when he would be sober. I just could not keep it to myself any longer!

It was a relief to find that Steve was not laughing. That hard-bitten *wallah* looked quite concerned as I explained in detail just what had happened during the past several evenings with Latifah.

"Young innocent, ain't you, Tiger? That game is as old as the hills. Betcha sweet life she's trying to get information out of you. Why, you're just the sort of kid these decoy dames would cotton on to, what with your straw-coloured mop and your blue lights. . . ."

"What has that to do with it, you fathead! "

"Now don't get your shirt out, Tiger. What I mean is, you've got that simple, friendly sort of look."

"Don't be an ass, Steve! These people have picked on me only because I happen to be doing batman to a political officer. They got to know that some way . . . I say! How did you find this dive in the first place?"

I had suddenly remembered that it was Steve who had led us there, just as if he had known the place before.

"I guess that's simple enough. Got the lowdown on the dive from an Arab in the *bazaar* coffee house. . . . Say, Tiger! Are you suggesting the whole thing was a plant? Was that Arab a decoy? Gee! I thought at the time the dirty *wallah* was being friendly!"

"Well," I said, "it begins to look that way. The fellow who's working those girls seem to have made up his mind to get me there. Having got me in the place, he leaves the rest to Latifah. It's all of a piece. Would you recognise that Arab again? "

The American stared hard for a minute.

"Come on," he snapped, "let's go!"

We went. We made straight for the coffee house in the *bazaar*. We drew a blank—which was what we might have expected. That Arabian, having played his part, was hardly likely to show up in that quarter again. Hanging around, searching the alleyways of the *bazaar*, peering at every passing Arab's jowl did us no good either. We gave up that line.

Evening found us once more at our favourite rendezvous, seeking solace among the pale-skinned damsels—though our interest in the place had considerably increased. Cockney Joe, who had also been made aware of the facts regarding Latifah, was of the opinion that we should run across the mysterious Arabian in the dive sooner or later. That seemed to be the excuse for frequenting the place night after night, for spending more time in the saloon and less with the girls.

We even essayed a little sleuthing through the passages that ran like warrens around the place. But we had to drop that line also. A narrow escape forced us to realise the error of such tactics. We must not arouse anyone's suspicions. Every other native in the place was a potential enemy. We might well ruin the whole thing by a too-precipitate action.

We went back to the girls. Latifah's attitude towards me did not waver. She was still concerned about losing me! She could not understand why I did not approach *le Capitan* and ask him whether I should leave Kut, and when; and was it true that many thousands of new soldiers were coming from my country to Iraq. If I loved as she loved, I would tell her these things and thus set her mind at rest. She would die if, not having been told, she waited one night for me and I did not come, *never* came again.

She could be so truly pathetic and appealingly childish about all this that I sometimes wondered if she were really concerned or just playing a part. Certainly she acted well. There were moments when the little wisp of a thing seemed utterly sincere, and I had all my work cut out not to betray myself. She made love as few women can. Maybe it was second nature to her. It became enormously difficult not to believe in her! Together on that pile of cushions . . . her soft murmurings . . . the world forgotten . . . only the enchanting whispers of night about us . . . how on earth did I refrain from taking her into my confidence?

I think she guessed something before the end. There was that in her attitude which was far above mere passion ... as if she really cared. I know I came perilously near to that state. After all, she was of the West as much as I. And one cannot get so very near to a woman without the woman being aware of one's sympathetic nearness. She betrayed as much. Once, with a shyness that was the sincerest part of her, she expressed the wish that we might go on and on for always. . . .

She offered me plans, half in play and half in earnest. I fancy she would have become very much in earnest if I had shown the least desire to fall in with any of her plans, if I should have considered anything so revolutionary as deserting from the British Army, in order to turn native until such times when we could flee from all this pother of war and slaughter and sudden death.

As a delightful dream, it was all very wonderful and very beautiful.. . .

But it was only a dream—born of sex and that mystic thing called woman.

And as a dream, it was rudely shattered. The bombshell was none of our making. It had nothing to do with Latifah or with me. Nor had it anything to do with my two pals. It came from a source entirely out of our reckoning.

Days went by, days of fatigues and parades and irksome duties and all the shiftless, aimless activities that mark the periods when a fighting force stands by, awaiting the next job of killing. True, there were minor killings. Shooting parties were turned out, Arabian prisoners were stood up against a wall, and—*phut!* We turned to the next job.

It was, curiously enough, a firing party that put "paid" to the Latifah episode. Steve and I were turned out early one morning with ten other men. We were lined up. Our rifles were inspected. We were told

that three Arabs awaited without. It was essential that our marksman-
ship should be true. Three natives had been convicted of misdemean-
ours that called for the death sentence.

It was my first experience in a firing party, and though I had seen
the sort of thing before, I did not fancy the cold-blooded job. There
was something grotesque in the way those three Arabs looked into
the face of death. Their attitude was nonchalant, sullen. The man in
the centre had a fist full of meat. He was chewing industriously. His
black eyes stared at the levelled rifles. They were expressive eyes. They
seemed to say—"Shoot and be damned! I am going to *Allah!*"

Twelve rifles barked simultaneously. The three prisoners crumpled
up. A chunk of meat, released from a relaxed fist, rolled into the dust.

But that was not all. As we were stowing our rifles, Steve clutched
at my arm. I was startled by the look in his face. I rarely saw him so
excited.

"Come outside—away from this mob!"

"Well," I said, when we had got out of earshot, "what's on?"

"Say! That Arab we shot! The fellow with his jaw full of meat!"

"What about him?"

"He's the dirty *wallah* that gave me the lowdown about Latifah's
show!"

"God in heaven! Are you sure?"

"Sure? I'll say I am! Would you ever mistake them lights of his,
having seen 'em once?"

"No. I don't think I should."

"Why, he hadn't even changed his clobber! That *burnous* of his—
striped like a sunblind. So what!"

"What were they convicted for?"

"Just so! I put that query to the corporal a couple of minutes ago.
They were convicted for espionage!"

"My God! Then Latifah . . . ?"

"Don't know, Tiger. How the hell should I know, anyway! We don't
shoot women, so what's your worry!"

"But this is ghastly. . . . Damn it all, Steve, I——"

"Yeah, I know. You feel for the kid."

I think I must have gone crazy just then. Luckily there was no one
within earshot or I should have been shoved into dock for inspection.
I fancy Steve, big as he was, had the dickens of a time holding me
down.

"Let go, damn you! I tell you I'm going down there to see!"

But Steve hung on, which was just as well for me. Blessings on that tough *wallah*. It was not the only time he saved me from being seriously crimed.

"Now pull yourself together, old fellah. We'll get down there right after dismissal this afternoon. There's the whistle! Come on, Tiger. Be a soldier!"

I don't know how I got through that day. I can only recall how Steve hung on to me, never let me out of his sight, pushing me through this job and that. It must have been patent to many that I had a touch of the sun. I had been more crazy about Latifah than I realised. Those endless hours were sheer torture. I suppose I behaved like an infatuated boy—which was precisely what I was.

When the hour of freedom came we went to that mysterious dive for the last time. It looked just the same as on other evenings. The place was full of natives, squatting on benches, smoking and drinking. The girls were flitting to and fro, indulging their friends, just as they had done every other evening when we had walked into the place. No one seemed to know, or care, whether certain members of the gang had been executed that day.

But I looked in vain for Latifah. She did not appear in the saloon. She was not in her own room. She was not anywhere in the building. The other girls did not know where she was—nor care. They merely shrugged their shoulders, then turned back to their amorous pursuits.

Many moons were to pass before I saw her again. There was a war on. We were to fight bloody battles—and lose them, take part in a tragic retreat, exist on starvation rations in a besieged Kut, face starvation, humiliation, surrender to the unspeakable Turk, kill our own horses for food, see men die of starvation at the rate of twenty a day, experience the tortures of hell—before I should see that lovely creature again.

CHAPTER 5

Battle of Ctesiphon

We made our trek from Kut to Ctesiphon by stages of route march, strenuous enough but not too exhausting, camping at some of the rendezvous in between—Umm al Tubul, Azizieh, El Kutunie, Zeur, Bustan and Lajj. The distance of that advance was ninety miles. We finally halted for the attack at Lajj, a short day's march from the Turkish position at Ctesiphon. We could see the famous arch of Ctesiphon in the distance. One thrilled to the sight of that giant arch. Some of the greatest battles of the world's history were fought on that historic ground.

That arch marks the spot of many a fight among princes and kings in the early days of civilisation. It has witnessed the charges of Assyrian chariots and the massed formation of Persian hordes. Cities, whose only relics today are a few scattered stones in the desert waste, were there besieged and defended, pillaged and plundered, sometimes by rival adjacent states, sometimes by the wild barbarians from the Steppes of Asia. . . . And now, nothing but a colossal arch of stone to tell of what was once the magnificent Audience Hall of the Parthians. . . .

And we were to stage a losing battle there! Of all places, at Ctesiphon, city of Babylonia, capital of the ancient Parthian kingdom, the city that was conquered by the Romans and destroyed by the Arabs under Omar, now a broken arch of stones and the site of one of the most ferocious battles in modern times.

We never dreamt then, when we advanced towards that giant piece of broken masonry, that we were to be the losers, that we should find ourselves involved in a gruelling retreat of ninety of the most miserable miles imaginable. We had advanced from our base at Basrah, winning every engagement for nearly three hundred miles along the Tigris to Kut. What was a mere ninety miles to Ctesiphon? And why should we suppose that fate had staged a grim laugh against us this time?

Everyone knows now that General Townshend was strongly opposed to that advance. He wished to stay at Kut until reinforcements could reach him from Egypt and France. He knew the miserable state of his land transport, the perilous condition of his lines of communications over that three hundred miles of flat desert, the unreliability of the small river transport and gunboats on account of the particularly tortuous and shallow state of the stream in this area. But he was overruled. The die was cast. He had to advance against his better judgement.

The troops began to move out of camp at Lajj for that historic battle in the afternoon of November 21, 1915. When darkness came the whole of the force, mainly composed of 9,000 infantry, was marching towards the Turkish trenches.

There were two aeroplanes operating at about this time. For several days before the battle started they had been preparing the way, making aerial reconnaissances of the enemy's position and the like. On November 13 one of these 'planes went out with the purpose of severing the telegraph line west of Baghdad, which linked the city with the Euphrates, the scheme being to isolate Nur-ud-din, the Turkish Commander, from Marshal von der Goltz, the German veteran of victories, who was hurrying down from Mosul, north of Baghdad, with reinforcements to relieve the Turks.

The observer in that 'plane was Major Yeats-Brown, who later was to become famous as the author of *Bengal Lancer*, and the inspirer of the film success, *The Lives of a Bengal Lancer*. Unfortunately for pilot and observer, their 'plane came to grief against a telegraph pole and in a few moments they were down in the desert and surrounded by hostile Arab horsemen. They were taken prisoners and saw no more of the war in Mesopotamia.

The other 'plane was piloted by Major Reilly, the brilliant and intrepid aviator who made such daring reconnaissances of the enemy's positions in the various advances of this campaign. He went out to cut telegraph wires too, on the eve of the battle of Ctesiphon. He did not return. Later it was learned that his machine came down. He was captured by the Arabs and handed over to the Turks. Thus, within a few hours of the battle, Major Townshend had lost the pilot whose work over several months had been invaluable.

The night before the battle was another night of forced marching that one cannot easily forget. Night marching is always trying, but marching and knowing that every step draws one nearer to the enemy's guns can be positively nerve-wracking. If only one could have the relief of a smoke! No smoking! No talking! "Quiet men!" On and on through the darkness—to heaven knows what! Shuffled about in columns! Placed in positions before the enemy's guns—on his front, on his left flank, rear of his left flank; for the position was to be much the same as at the Battle of Kut. . . .

We were in position by daylight. Nothing happened. I was with the column that was to make the flanking movement as before. It wasn't a pleasant prospect—even if it succeeded. . . . That ghastly business of bombarding trenches from behind. Besides, how should we know that Johnny wasn't waiting for us this time with some trick of his own? There were rumours, too, that he was being strongly reinforced, that he outnumbered us by several thousands. We knew he had been building his redoubts and entrenchments for months. On the left flank his trenches extended for six miles northwards from the river.

As for my own impressions during those hectic minutes when we were preparing to storm his trenches—all I could see was a vast expanse of desert with the imposing arch of Ctesiphon towering up as a landmark for many miles around, with groups of tombs about it, including the historic tomb of Salman Pak, the tomb of a devoted servant of the prophet Mahomet and a very holy place in the eyes of the Mahommedans. That, incidentally, was a great source of trouble among certain sections of Townshend's army, for we had many Mahommedans among the Indian units, and they were not exactly anxious to fight their brother Mahommedans among the Turks. Moreover, they openly refused to fight near the holy ground which marked the spot of the tomb of Salman Pak.

> In this connection, (said General Townshend), I had to send back to Basrah one Indian battalion, composed in the bulk of trans-border men of the North West of India, owing to numerous cases of desertion to the enemy. It was a danger to my force, and I declined to have it any longer in my command.

This at a time when every available man was needed! No one appeared to be troubling much about Mesopotamia at this time. Certainly there was no question of reinforcing the little army that had done so much since its original landing in a strange land a year previously.

Four days before this battle opened Sir John Nixon heard from the British War Office in London that Von der Goltz had left Baghdad on November 10, and that 30,000 Turks were marching from Antolia to their Mesopotamian front. Sir John replied that for more than a fort-night his own agents had been giving him similar news. He just did not accept these reports as conclusive. Yet, when it was all over, it was General Townshend, who was opposed to this advance, who came in for all the knocks.

The battle started at eight o'clock on that memorable morning, November 22, 1915. As the Irishman said (proudly)—"We began it." It seemed that Johnny Turk was content to sit in his trenches and wait for us to come right up to his guns, wait for us to open fire in fact. We did. We got a roar of guns and a rattle of musketry in reply. Soon it seemed that all the world was filled with belching cannon, the chattering and stuttering of machine guns, and the splutter of rifles. Our opening was the signal for the whole line of entrenched Turks to vomit their hot lead from six miles of trenches.

The uproar was deafening, the fire continually increasing in vio-lence and intensity. It may be clever tactics to manoeuvre men so that they fold over an enemy's flank, but for the Tommies participating in such a game it is a regular hell-corner. We poured withering fire into the trenches from the rear. One's blood raced with excitement and the feverish pressing of clips, firing, running forward, ducking, firing, running, taking a thousand chances. There was a determined attempt this time to beat us off, but how could those entrenched men face both ways!

They would swing round, reaching up to us—which was fatal! Exposed heads were knocked over like dummies on some crazy Aunt Sally stall. *Phut!* And a bleeding head would disappear behind a trench wall. This terrible menacing of their line of retreat caused large num-bers of the Turks to abandon the first line and fall back on the second. We jumped in, trampling down dead and wounded in our excitement. The enemy could be seen retreating in masses. We yelled with passion and heat at the sight!

And then we had a shock! The great mass of Turks who had fallen back on the second line now stood their ground. Once he is well en-trenched, the Turk is as ferocious a fighter as any soldier in the world. They seemed to be standing shoulder-to-shoulder in that section of the trenches which directly faced us. Though we filled their trenches with bullets and bombs, they remained firm as rocks.

I shall never forget our wild charge on that particular section. Right in front of me was a tangled bunch of barbed wire and spread over it like a man crucified, his sightless eyes turned up to heaven, was one of our Indian troops. His eyes had been gouged out before he was pitched from the point of a bayonet on to that barbed wire. I don't know if he still breathed. I do know that an officer, racing past, paused for a split second and fired his revolver full in the man's face.

Men yelled dirty oaths at the sight of that horrible thing. Johnny Turk paid for it many times over in the next half hour. Many of the Turks fought desperately, hand-to-hand. Others left their trenches in flight. Dead and wounded lay sprawled about everywhere—our own as well as the enemy's. In some places the dead lay so thickly together that we had difficulty in keeping our feet amongst them.

Yet, there was no doubt about it, the enemy was making a strong stand for the second position. The retreat was spasmodic, not general. Whole companies were being annihilated . . . and then another massed horde of them would roll up in front of us. We knew then that Johnny had a strong reserve. As the day advanced and the fighting grew more and more fierce, the unbelievable fact was forced upon us that our crazy 400-miles advance from Basrah to Ctesiphon was being checked, that this might well be our first reverse—*we*, who had conquered all the way!

Something had gone wrong! That was one's first vague impression. The attacking columns became muddled. There were times when I found myself among a bunch of Indian troops, fighting side by side with them; and not I alone, but hundreds of others were doing the same thing. Then I realised that there were no officers in our immediate neighbourhood. Johnny had taken a heavy toll. That accounted for our disorderly fighting. The N.C.O.'s were yelling themselves hoarse in their efforts to get us into something like formation, but an N.C.O. has not the pulling power of an officer.

I think a great many of us went stark raving mad then. There was a certain thought in the minds of all of us that kept us going through those frightful hours of slaughter, that stimulated our superhuman endurance it was the terror of being left in the hands of the Turks, or worse still, the Arabs. We were all old and hardened warriors by this time and we knew what to expect of our Moslem enemy, be he Turk or Arabian—a slit throat, a belly full of stones, unspeakable outrages by pederastic brown men upon the white *infidels*, sadistic mutilations under the hands of their brown women. When a man knows these things, he will fight like one possessed, fight until he drops—which was what many hundreds of our boys did—rather than be caught. . . . It was not heroism, courage, the intrepid fighting spirit. It was none of those things. It was sheer terror of what might happen to one.

Men voiced these things as they fought.

"Come on, you brown bastards! You don't get me for a game. . . ."

And come on they did, in all conscience. Line after line of them rose up in those reserve trenches. These were men fresh to the game. That was obvious. They fought like fresh soldiers. By noon of that day we had to realise that Johnny Turk was making a counter-offensive in an attempt to throw us off his second position.

In a wild charge, thoroughly uncontrolled and without any specific order that I can remember, we took a large section of the enemy's second line. Our troops were hurriedly installing themselves. Those trenches were piled high with bodies. The stench was appalling. Foul oaths were tossed about in several languages. Reeking blood under a blazing sun had turned men into beasts. It seemed there were no officers left among us anymore—and that leaves a Tommy in a queer state of mind. I know that, for a brief space with us, it was a case of every man for himself and to hell with Johnny. That was all that filled our horizon then, annihilate Johnny Turk or—something worse than death for us.

In the end we were bombed out of those trenches again. There could be no question about the enemy being heavily reinforced. The casualties among the officers were so great that men turned round de-liberately and went back with our wounded! The Indians were turn-ing round and walking back in bunches, but not only Indian troops, British as well! The victory we had won over the enemy's first and second positions was slowly slipping from us.

Soon hundreds of Indian soldiers were streaming away towards our rear. They had lost practically all their British officers. For the want of a few reinforcements we were losing a great victory. It was appall-ing but true. Men turned as they fought, bawling at those who were running away, naming them for every sort of adjectival coward. Then a bunch of our "redcaps" (staff officers) came racing up and literally pushed the men back into the battle! They raced about restoring or-der, punching laggards, driving men into line, joining themselves in the combat, encouraging others with their behaviour, keeping men in hand with stern words of command, fighting side by side with the men they had restored to us.

They saved us from an uncontrolled retreat and the consequent demoralising rout. And it was all done under heavy fire and at the most critical stage of the battle. The voice of authority had prevailed and discipline was restored. But I shall never forget it. That dribbling of men to the rear might have developed into a disorderly and wholesale retreat with the enemy on our heels and with no proper base on which to fall back, *for Kut was ninety miles away.*

All of Tommy Atkins' training tends to foster the belief in his British invincibility, and it is just this traditional swagger that stands him in good stead whenever he is in a tight corner. Defeat is not in his category. When he is up against an overwhelming force and is driven back—well, it is merely a temporary setback!

Those staff officers rallied numbers of men by word of command. They animated the troops to hold out against intimidating hordes by their example, and many of them went down in the scrimmage. The fire became more violent than ever. Shells were screaming over our heads. We were compelled to fall back again, but this time in a solid and ordered formation.

Then the Turks retook the guns we had captured—not that they were any use to them, for we had removed the breech-blocks! Other of our units came up in support. We must hold on to the Turks' first line at all costs! We did! Heaven knows how. For now it was late afternoon and we were pretty well spent. We had been in it since eight of the morning without a pause.

When night fell on that memorable twenty-second of November we were still in possession of the battlefield. How thankful we were for the darkness! We dropped in our tracks, literally gasping with exhaustion. I don't know what happened then. I knew vaguely that Johnny was still sending an occasional shell over, that men were moving about me in the darkness, carrying back the wounded on stretchers. ... I fell asleep. A long night of marching followed by an even longer day of the most strenuous and ferocious battle had been too much for me. I slept where I lay and if Johnny had come along I should not have known. He could have had me for the taking. I was too exhausted to care anymore.

I believe I was left alone for about three hours in that muddle of a night—though it seemed like three minutes to me—and then I was dragged to my feet. I fell in automatically with a party of men in much the same condition as myself. Somebody was dishing out shovels. I stared rather stupidly at the implement, I suppose. . . .

"We ain't killing 'em with shovels, Tiger. This is a funeral party. Come on, be a soldier! "

So we went around burying our dead and collecting identity discs so that mothers and wives and relatives at home could be advised that Dick, Tom and Harry had been "killed in action" at Ctesiphon. Only it did not work out quite like that. We dug holes and threw in bodies, arms, legs, and other bits and pieces, filling them in as quickly as we knew how. What sort of funeral could anybody hope for after such a day? All fire had died down. One supposed that Johnny was burying *his* dead. It was a gruesome job in that blackness, a perfect end to a perfect day. It made one think—coming as we did upon odds and ends of limbs, bodies with heads almost severed. . . . Some of our fellows had been blown to bits. . . . The great concern seemed to be identity discs.

In official jargon, the night of the twenty-second and twenty-third was spent in rallying our forces and burying our dead and evacuating the wounded. That day we lost 4,000 killed and wounded out of 8,500 bayonets. When daylight came we were installed in trenches once more. The orders were to "make good the position we had won." It was hoped that the Turks would retreat during the night—"when their wounds got stiff."

We discovered that Johnny had retreated a little way. He was behind the Diala River, which flows into the Tigris at this point. But he was by no means beaten. He was preparing to give battle again from his new vantage point, and that could only mean he was being efficiently reinforced. Whilst we, who must hold what we had, had been reduced to nearly half our original number.

Added to which, there was neither food nor water—except what was left of the iron rations and the bottle of water we had been given on the evening of the 21st! Maybe that was why we shifted our position nearer the river and under the shadow of the gigantic Arch of Ctesiphon. We dug in behind the "high walls of Ctesiphon," which are not walls at all but high mounds, built probably at the time of the Roman conquest.

The evacuation of the wounded and the movements of troops went on throughout the whole of that day. Just what all the re-shuffling was about we could not guess. Doubtless the powers-that-be had their own ideas. To us troops it appeared that we were making many futile movements that day. And all the time the wounded were being passed along—mainly in springless carts drawn by mules, which must have been excruciating torture for broken limbs and splintered backs.

[1] At Basra we had met men who had been at Ctesiphon. We heard of wounded who had been carried nine miles from the battlefield to the ship in these carts. They are springless, made of wood and iron bars with a gridiron bottom, ordinarily employed for the carriage of equipment or supplies. Every jolt in them over this broken ground was like a deliberate blow; men with broken arms and legs were condemned in them to a prolonged agony. Generally there were no mattresses. To a twice-wounded man, who had made the journey before, they must have seemed like the tumbrils of the Revolution. To be consigned to one after haemorrhage or with a wound in the stomach or about the spine meant death. Every doctor who packed such a case in the A.T. carts knew the man's fate as certainly as if he had signed his death-warrant. Yet these carts were tolerated in Mesopotamia as the normal ambulance conveyance for nearly two years.

Night fell again and we were still evacuating the wounded. Johnny had been quiet all day. Maybe he had been too busy with his wounded and the consolidating of his position. It was a very dark night, and it looked as if we were to be left in peace to rest after our labours. What was left of the Slaughtering Seventh was in position behind the mounds, which was the reserve. Troops were entrenched ahead of us. We had ceased to be the storming troops, for there was no storm left in us.

It was an eerie experience to lie there, staring at the giant shape of the Arch, and to reflect that on this very ground, behind these same "high walls," the Roman soldiers had fought desperately to recover Mesopotamia from the Persians. Should we recover Ctesiphon from the Turks? I don't think any of us had much hope then.

Johnny was not to leave us in peace. His guns began again about eight o'clock that night. Shells burst over the trenches, stabbing the darkness with flashes of light. Then they came, black masses of them, advancing towards our first line with a roar of musketry. As fast as one black mass was driven off another took its place. The tables were turned with a vengeance. The Turks were now making the offensive and we a desperate defence. On they came, one group after another, attacking with the utmost fury. One after another they were repulsed,

---

1. *The Long Road To Baghdad*, by Edmund Candler.

but at times they almost forced their way into our trenches.

At one part of the line the Turks actually got into our trenches—only to be bombed out again, leaving numbers of dead and wounded behind. All this we could see from our reserve position behind the mounds, for the night was sometimes ablaze with explosives. The expenditure of ammunition, and especially the Turkish shells, must have been enormous. Evidence indeed of the fresh supplies and fresh men for the enemy.

There was an occasion when it became touch-and-go. Why the Turks did not storm all over us and take us all prisoners must be one of those inexplicable mysteries of war. They swung round in great groups on our flanks. The Indians deserted their trenches and raced back towards the reserve, which left the Turks in possession—but not for long. They hesitated to advance further and so lost the opportunity to sweep over the whole of our earthworks. Before they could rally for the final sweep a number of our troops were rushed to the flank, driving the Indians back with them. Johnny saw the manoeuvre as a counter-attack—when it was merely a desperate attempt to regain the flank entrenchments—and fled!

It was about three o'clock in the morning before the attacks died down and we could breathe freely once more. Then there was more work for the Slaughtering Seventh. We were turned out from behind those mounds and sent up the lines to collect the wounded and bury the dead. We went with rumbling mule carts, carrying ammunition up to the front line and bringing back the wounded.

It was something of a nerve-strain in that thick gloom, for we never knew just when Johnny might take it into his head to creep around and start the fun all over again. The squeak and rumble of the wretched carts could be heard a mile away, now that the firing had ceased, and it must have taxed the enemy's patience and ingenuity to figure out just what we were doing there in the darkness. It maybe that he mistook the rumbling wheels of our wagons for the movements of gun limbers, in which case he must have thought we were bringing up fresh guns. Heavens! If only we had had a few to bring up—to say nothing of a few fresh men! For we still had him guessing. And in that state it would have required but a small reinforcement to lick him. Had he known the true state of the British force, he must surely have annihilated us!

When the morning of the twenty-fourth dawned we discovered that Johnny had retired under cover of the darkness. He was nowhere in sight! He had gone back to his snuggery behind the River Diala. That morning we evacuated all our wounded and transferred them to boats on the river, to be convoyed downstream. The force was rallied round the high walls near the Arch. It looked pitifully small. We were served with fresh rations of bully beef and bread and heard the welcome cry of "*Char up!*" That tea was nearly black, hardly sweetened at all, and without milk, but it was nectar to us! The meal heartened us beyond belief. The effect upon the men of that good square meal and that swig of tea was positively astonishing. Our spirits rose. We laughed and joked and bantered together. Forgotten were those two ghastly days of slaughter and gruesome labours. We were new men!

That day was fairly quiet. The Turks' guns shelled us intermittently, and though the Arch made a good mark for our position, there were very few casualties. It would seem appropriate to interject a little of one's diary at this stage:

November 24, 1915.—Am writing in the shadow of the Arch of Ctesiphon. Resting after more than two days of hell. There ought to be an air of tension, a fearful straining of the senses, a querying as to what Johnny Turk will do next—and when! But there isn't. Only too relieved at this respite. Men all around me sitting in sun delousing. Our temporary occupation of Johnny's trenches gave us many specimens Oriental variety. Hot argument as I write as to who has biggest lice. Fight ensues. Prime specimens of Oriental lice are lost. A beauty the size of housefly jumps on my paper and off again. Great occasion for mirth at Tiger's expense. . . . Unholy scramble for the louse. . . . An N.C.O. rolls up. More fatigue. Evacuating wounded still. Poor devil on stretcher with tummy like a woman in family way. They say it is some virulent disease the fellow picked up from Turkish prisoners. Rude remarks from delousing Tommies about Johnny's pederastic proclivities. . . . Appalling how men can get used to sight of death and wounds—and still joke. No wonder Babylon fell. Our aeroplane comes down near G.H.Q. He has been on reconnaissance of enemy's position. Now we shall hear something. Discussion is rife. Boys think we are finished. Couldn't stand another attack. . . .

And we were finished. There was a big movement towards the river that night. It was followed by another more or less quiet day, though Johnny kept on pitching his shells around. November 25 found us cleaning up, moving stores and ammunition dumps. We were to fall back on Lajj. Obviously we were in retreat. There was nothing at Lajj to help us—just entrenchments. We had these at Ctesiphon. What was the point in falling back on Lajj?

We started at about nine o'clock that night. Not a single shot followed us. It was a perfectly orderly retreat. We might have been on a route march in Blighty—except that we knew we were retreating. That required a lot of swallowing for troops that had advanced over three hundred miles. As I recall it, it certainly did not help to raise our spirits. There was a lot of talk about the move being a temporary measure in order to give our reinforcements time to catch up with us. But that did not go down well either. We knew how far it was from Basrah. We landed there a year ago. There were no railways to bring up the reinforcements to us. They would have to come the way we did—on boats and barges as far as they could, but hot-footing for the most part.

These weren't very jolly reflections for us now that we were going backwards! Some wag started to sing improvised lines about the Forgotten Army—until an officer shut him up with a few red-blood epithets.

My section was in the rearguard of that march, which is always a rotten position. The Arab horsemen rolled up in the early hours and started spraying us with lead. It is a habit of such dirty cowards. Their idea of fun—hanging around the rearguard of a retreating column and taking pot-shots. It got too much for us in the end. Orders were given to turn about and charge them.

It was a lovely fight! Just the sort we were spoiling for in the mood of the moment. We suddenly broke loose upon these Arabs—who had dismounted in order to come in close. We fell upon them, while the column marched on. It was a regular father and mother of a scrap. Our onslaught was so unexpected that they were taken unawares. We had about a score of them surrounded in no time at all. And then the fireworks. Those we did not shoot were battered to death with rifle-butts. Not one of them was left standing. A whistle blew. We fell in and doubled back to the column. We reached the main body breathless but triumphant!

There was a *communiqué* issued to the troops regarding this fall back upon Lajj, which is worth quoting:

Sir John Nixon has expressed in his Army Order his sentiments in the very words I would have chosen myself. I cannot express my admiration and gratitude for the heroism displayed by all ranks. To show with what stern valour you fought, you drove four divisions out of a very strong position and forced them to retire beyond the Diala river. But our numbers were too few to put them to rout; we have had 4,000 men killed and wounded, the Turks losing many more than this figure. You have added a brilliant page to the glorious battle roll of the Army in India, and you will be proud to tell them at home that you fought at the battle of Ctesiphon.

The troops must know that I have ordered a move back to Lajj for the following reasons:

Food and supply question. The ships are exposed to fire on the river at Bustan, and the enemy can with cavalry accompanied by guns stop their progress up river to opposite this camp.

At Lajj I can await in security the arrival of reinforcements at Basra from France and Egypt, due in a week's time.

The ships at Lajj are in security.

Three monitors are promised to me in a few days.

Reinforcements in a week's time! Somebody had been terribly misinformed. They did not arrive for months! And then it was too late! Food and supplies. We did not know then, when we marched through the night to fall back on Lajj, that we should eventually fall back on Kut ninety miles away and there be conquered by famine!

The morning of November 26 found us at Lajj, in a miserable drizzle of rain, depressed, weary, sick to death of the rotten war in Mesopotamia, ready to fly at the throat of any prize ass who dared to murmur optimistically about those reinforcements coming up from Basrah. For we knew then—as soldiers always do know these things—that the fall back upon Lajj was but a step in the retreat down the long weary road we had fought so hard to gain. We had no faith in those "ships" on the river, in either the question of support or supply. We had had too much experience of the treacherous Tigris—that winds like a writhing snake through the land that is so inaptly called "the cradle of civilisation."

CHAPTER 6

Retreat!

We dug in at Lajj and slept in the sand holes which rapidly turned into mud troughs under that persistent drizzle of rain. But there appeared to be no real attempt to entrench ourselves—which could only mean one thing, we were not to stay at Lajj. It was, of course, the first step in the retreat, though we did not know it then. We did not know much. But evidently the generals knew. One of General Nixon's dispatches at this time is most revealing:

> During the afternoon large columns were seen advancing down the left bank, and also inland as if to turn our flank, while hostile cavalry threatened our rear. General Townshend was nine miles from his shipping and source of supplies at Lajj, faced by superior forces of fresh troops.

Yet we were told we were falling back on Lajj in order to be near our food and supplies.

Anyway, there was every possibility of Lajj camp being under water before long, so we got out. Which was just as well. Our air reconnaissance learned that the advance guard of the Turkish force, numbering about 15,000, had left Ctesiphon and was advancing on Lajj. On the afternoon of November 27 we hot-footed to Azizieh in one march of twenty-two miles. We were caked with mud, fed to the back teeth, and weary beyond description.

Men dropped by the roadside and were thrown into mule carts. The enemy, a massed force big enough to wipe us out of the country altogether, was almost treading on our heels. We hoofed it through the night by way of Zeur and El Kutunie, and if there is anything more miserable than the retreat of an army that has advanced victoriously for a year—I should not like to meet it. When we reached Azizieh we were put to work! All the wounded had to be evacuated on steamers and barges, *and all our stores were being sent down the river.* . . .

It soon became a question as to who would get to Kut first—Johnny or us! Even while we were at Azizieh we learned that the enemy had a column a mile long in occupation of El Kutunie, six miles away. We could hear his big guns shelling one of our steamers that had stuck on the river bank. For days then we lived in a state of constant readiness, sleeping when and how we could, fully dressed and fully equipped, nursing our rifles and cursing our disciples.

We left Azizieh in a hurry. There was not time to load all our stores on the barges—clothing and equipment and an ammunition dump. We left a column of belching smoke behind, which must have been very amusing to Johnny only six miles away at El Kutunie! In the afternoon of that day (November 30) we arrived at Umm-ul-Tubul. The river craft with wounded, stores and ammunition rolled up shortly afterwards; but owing to the state of the stream it was impossible for the steamers and barges to carry on through the night. *So the retreating army stayed where it was in order to guard the river craft that held its only means of subsistence!* Such was the state of the transport in the Mesopotamian Campaign after a year in the country.

"Well, I guess that gives us a break," opined Steve. "We'll get a rest and a good dose of shut-eye, maybe."

But Steve had to guess again. We passed an anxious night, as they say in polite circles. A brigade had been sent on ahead of us. They were some ten miles away when messengers went off to bring 'em back again. They had to double back those ten miles. At least, I could be thankful I was not in that crush. Johnny started to shell us about ten pip emma, and we needed every available man to help us out of the muddle into which the guarding of our own transport had landed us.

We could hear the distant rumble of the enemy's gun-limbers. Then the fireworks. The shells started splashing hot lead all around us. It was a lively situation for tired Tommies in the dead darkness of night. At one time it looked as if we should be taken by the collar while guarding our ships. There was little we could do in that inky blackness. Nobody seemed to know whether this was the advance guard or whether the whole force of Turks was surrounding us. God! How we prayed for daylight! From mid- night onwards every man was in his place, on his feet, standing in the ranks, first on one leg and then on the other tired one. Were we ready to move off or move into battle—which?

Came the dawn—of the first day in December. And what a dawn! Fifteen thousand Turks were moving towards us in a great extended line that seemed to stretch over the desert as far as the eye could reach. Their artillery was at close field-gun range—about 2,000 yards away. The sight was positively terrifying. It was not so much the enemy's overwhelming force that awed us. We were tired. Heavens! What a world of meaning there is in that word! We were numb and sick with weariness.

With the first splash of dawn our guns began belching fire. We went up behind them, believing this was the end. From being tired and sick we became incredibly heated and lusting for blood. At least, we could give 'em hell before they *did* take us. I had made up my mind that I would not be taken alive, and I fancy my state was pretty general.

Granted such a body of infuriated men, what is likely to ensue? Even as we rushed towards Johnny's left wing that was doing its damndest to envelop us, our artillery was annihilating lines of men with their 18-pounders. That shattering gunfire paralysed the advancing lines. We saw them hesitate, come to a wobbling kind of halt. It only needed the menace of our cavalry—Indian, and British hussars, to turn that hesitation into a bolt! I have never seen such a wild, ungovernable dash as those cavalry boys made, Indians and British mixed. It was the most inspiriting thing that could have happened to us. Then the horse artillery were also in action behind a ridge away out beyond the enemy's flank. One could see shells and shrapnel bursting all over the place. In a few moments Johnny's enveloping attack upon us had become a rout. He *had* turned tail. The Turk is as good as any soldier in the world when he is securely entrenched. In the open he hasn't the guts of a louse. With such overpowering numbers he ought to have wiped our little force off the face of the earth. Instead of which, he bolted. Soon the whole of his lines were turning about and running hither and thither in the craziest disorder.

Under his retreat we rallied for the charge. But it was not to be. We were not the attackers any more. We fell back *en échelon*, moving to the word of command like men on a parade ground. We were still under heavy shell fire. In his story of the campaign, General Townshend has written of this particular movement:

We were under very heavy shell fire; but I have never seen— even in peace manoeuvres—a retirement carried out better, both as regards steadiness and suppleness in manoeuvre, than was executed by the Sixth Division at this critical moment. The sight of the brigades falling back steadily in *echelon*, with the precision of clockwork, and the gradual development into one steady flow of retreat in perfect order—guns, everything, in their proper places—filled me with pride. Shall I ever have such a command again, I thought?

We fought in that amazing action from dawn until about eight of the morning. Johnny did not take a single prisoner from us. And we hung on to the 1,500 prisoners we had taken at Ctesiphon and who were marching with our column in the retreat. Nor did we lose a single gun. We, however, lost about 500 men in killed and wounded. It should be mentioned, too, that the brigade that had been sent on ten miles ahead of us and then dragged back again, and which had done some eighty miles in all in the past three days, fought during that astounding dawn engagement with the same spirit of doggedness as the rest of the army!

In this engagement at Umm-el-Tubul the enemy brought his guns up to within fifty yards of two of our gunboats on the river—the *Comet* and the *Firefly*, both of which we lost. The *Firefly* was the same gunboat that had sent three men ashore at Amarah early in the campaign to take the surrender of the enemy at that town, and she was recaptured when, in February, 1917, the British force advanced on Baghdad—retaken at almost the same spot where she was lost on that memorable morning.

We started marching again, continuing all that day and half the night. Men were falling out from sheer exhaustion and bundled into carts. We dared not leave any behind for the Arabs were potting at our rear incessantly and we knew what would happen to the men they picked up. We had seen evidences of their handiwork on many occasions when we were advancing and Johnny Turk was dropping behind. That fact always astonished us—that these Arab Moslems should indulge in mutilations upon their brother Moslems the Turks!

It was about ten o'clock that night when we reached Shadie. I don't know now how we kept going all that day and half that night. *We fought an engagement at dawn and then marched thirty-six miles!* If I live to be a hundred, I shall never forget that march. I should have been in the cart too, if it had not been for Steve. I dozed as I staggered along. Towards the end I was being dragged along and Steve was carrying my rifle and most of my equipment as well as his own, and cursing me soundly for a Cissy. I would not like to repeat his language, but I had got to the stage when I did not care what happened. I gave in. . . .

When the order came to halt at Shadie, we dropped in ranks, the whole column, and slept like logs in the roadway. We did not want food. As a matter of historical fact, there wasn't any food. We had marched all day and half the night without. At daylight we stood on our stiffened legs and started to march again, *still without food*. It was kept up without a halt until one pip emma, with the Arabs following us and taking pot-shots the whole time. If we could have got hold of some of those dirty brown fellows we should, in our state, have been able to teach them something about mutilation. It is astonishing just how much the human frame will stand. We surely broke all records on that march. "*An army marches on its stomach.*" Ours must have been a pretty flat march!

We halted at one o'clock of that day for two hours. Still no food. There was, however, the cheerying news that food was being sent out to the column from Kut—provided we marched to Shumran Bend, some six miles or so from the town. We did. That last lap very nearly killed us. We must have presented a terrible picture, war-worn, weary, unshaven, caked with mud, a column of soldiers staggering along like drunken men.

I insisted on carrying my own rifle and equipment, in spite of all Steve's protests—who had the endurance of an ox—for I felt Kut was very near now. I filled my mind with the thoughts of Kut. And how could I think of Kut without picturing Latifah? I am sure it was only the vision of her that kept me on my feet. She may have been merely a Circassian girl without a moral to her back. To me she was the love-liest thing one could hope to meet in that benighted, God-forsaken country. Over and over again those last few torturing hours, when my feet dragged, my legs stiffened, and my back was one solid ache, I would picture her in that room with the pile of cushions where the lamp burned dimly, where there was ease and comfort and love and sloth and what could only be luxury to me.

Maybe I talked, or gabbled, or wandered in a sort of delirium. I don't know. I was conscious only of wooden limbs and leaden feet— and the joyous bundle I'd once had in my arms. And would again!

"You're crazy, Tiger! You're stark, raving loopy! Pull yourself to-gether, for the love of Mike! If anybody hears you ranting about that blasted dame—well, observation ward for you, old fellah. Come on, pick 'em up! Be a soldier and stop slobbering like a pink tea!"

Thus friend Steve, only in more sanguinary language.

"When I find her . . . I'm going to get away from this life of hell."

"Sure, the boy's nuts! Where'd you go, you crazy little runt, in a country like this—out'n the desert for the brown fellahs to get the pair of you?"

"She knows the country."

"I'll say she does! Knows it so well she wouldn't take a chance with you or any other white-skinned blighter."

"You don't know her as well as I."

"And that's no loss to me. . . . You crazy young pup! Ain't you got anything under your topee besides the roots of your hair? Guess you'll feel better after some chow. . . . Anyway, how'n hell you going to find the dame? She may be conked out by now."

"In either event, I've finished soldiering."

"Is that so!"

I had quite made up my mind. I had had all the shot and shell and mud and blood that any youngster could stand. I was through. I thought only of Latifah. I knew she'd do what I wanted to do. We'd get under cover until all this fighting and trekking and starving was over. Just then I was not troubling about the why and wherefore. Mere details had no place in my dreams. In times of severe stress you cannot keep a young and imaginative temperament at bay.

There was Persia, for instance, not very many miles away. Persia with all its beauty and colour, all the mysticism and glamour of the East! There were gardens of paradise there! Who would choose war when he could have love? Besides, I was busy picturing Latifah when she laughed—the most wonderful sight, the most pleasing sound in my cramped experience. . . .

"*The runt is light-headed!*" quoth Steve.

"A flask of wine and thou . . . this wilderness were paradise enow!"

"Aw, stow it! For the love of Pete! Pick 'em up, Tiger! We'll be at the Shumran Bend in a few minutes. . . . Sure, kid! And then for some eats, huh?"

"Who'd stay in this grey-desert . . . seething and sullen, reeking with blood and filth. . . ."

"Say, Tiger! If you don't lay off, I'll burst you!"

And so on and so on, until I fell asleep at Shumran Bend.

And yet, my case was nothing compared to some. We linked up

with Cockney Joe again at Kut. He was one of the details who had helped to guard a barge full of wounded from Shadie. A squadron of Turkish cavalry had caught them up and had sprayed them with machine-gun fire, wounded and all. The wounded and the fit were killed in heaps as they lay or stood about the steel deck of the barge. Men screamed when their wounds were shot at afresh. Panic ensued. Men with broken limbs fell overboard and were used as targets by the enemy. The barge ran aground and was boarded by the yelling Turks. In a few minutes the steel decks were running with blood. The Cockney swore that he saw men cut up before his very eyes. . . . Saw parts tossed into the air by the lust-drunken Turks and Arabs. . . .

In the end there was nothing to do but run for it. The dozen or so who remained standing at the end of a blood-thirsty half-hour had no option but to jump ashore and race along the old desert road as fast as they could go. They ran from sheer terror of what they had seen, and they kept on running for hours. Only seven of them reached the column. The fate of the others, fallen by the wayside, cannot be imagined. They were never seen again. It is to be hoped they died of exhaustion before the natives reached them with their knives. Poor Cockney Joe was never the same man.

We marched into Kut early in the morning of December 3, 1915. Perhaps it would be more correct to say that we crawled into the town. The Arab population eyed us sullenly, contemptuously. We were the beaten army, beaten in every sense of the word. They knew quite well why we had retreated back to their town. It was written all over us for everyone to see. Beaten! The Mesopotamian Arab is a merciless and cowardly dog. If the natives of Kut had had sufficient arms and ammunition they would have driven us from their town; but, beaten as we were, we still presented a too hefty proposition. Besides, we had all our guns, stores and ammunition. We moved in *en masse*, with quite plenty of material to carry on the war for some little time! It has since been proved that ours was the most orderly and efficacious retreat of modern military history. General Townshend wrote of this retreat in his book:

> On December 1st I was forced to halt and to fight against my will, in order to save some ships and barges on the river. Yet not only was the attack repulsed, but it was driven headlong back by means of an offensive counter-stroke on the enemy's flank, which all experienced soldiers will recognise as sufficient testi-

mony to the discipline and manoeuvring powers of the troops in retreat. After repulsing the enemy I broke off the action—the hardest test of all in rearguard fighting—and continued the retirement in *echelons* of brigades, under as good conditions as in peace training. Not a single wounded man was left behind, though 500 were killed and wounded in that action; not a single gun was lost, and 1,500 Turkish prisoners marched with my column throughout. Never, I consider, has a British force done longer or more exhausting marches than those of 1st and 2nd December. (Thirty-six and forty miles!) Never in any war in modern military history have British troops been more highly tried than in the Ctesiphon operations. Yet, never was there a murmur—never the slightest sign of demoralisation or insubordination. I hope that history will call this also an honourable retreat.

CHAPTER 7

Back in Kut

"Gosh! Could you think of a better way to search for Latifah? Could you, Steve!"

"Nope. You crazy loon! I could not!" The order had gone forth that every house in Kut must be searched for arms! For two days after our arrival in the town most of us had done nothing but sleep and eat. Now the exhausted army was getting on its feet again. We were trenching around the old mud fort, to the north and the north east, for the rest we were more or less protected by the loop of the Tigris. As thus:

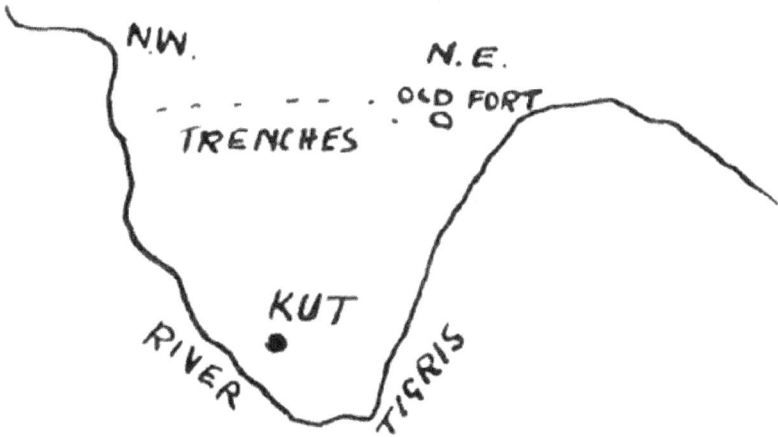

NATIVE WOMEN BEFORE THE DAYS OF STARVATION SET IN!

I was lucky enough to be in one of the detachments detailed to search the houses for firearms. Apart from the fact that it was the best possible way to search for Latifah, it was the most revealing insight regarding the habits and customs of the Arabian in his own home I've ever experienced—and I have spent many years in Arabia since then.

True, there was some looting in a friendly sort of way. I've seen worse. Some of the householders received us sullenly, some indifferently, some with snarls and mutterings, and some with *kow-towing* obeisances. It was all very amusing and not a little exciting. And for me, there was always the possibility of finding Latifah in the next house. The Christian element was easy enough. They had nothing to hide from us. They really desired us as masters in this strange country.

There were Arabs who adopted a friendly attitude too, offering us food, drink, cigarettes. When the Arabian becomes hospitable, he will take a lot of beating. His hospitality can be a trifle embarrassing, as when he offers one the use of his couch and one of his black-eyed wenches. And as soldiers go—they went. It was not uncommon for a party, reaching the more secluded apartments of a dwelling, to come upon a comrade in arms, very much in arms.

The procedure was simple enough. We hammered on the door, then thrust our way in. They were nearly always ready for us. The news would spread by way of the bazaars. Watching women and staring children would stand about while we turned over bedding and upset furniture. We found very little in the way of firearms. The Arab, male and female, wears voluminous clothing. It was not much good searching the houses and ignoring the householders; but mostly it was the women who secreted the stuff, and in the most extraordinary places. Also it was quite clear that they were accustomed to these searchings. As soon as we entered some of the houses the womenfolk would adopt a prone position with their clouts above their heads. Apparently such gestures of tacit submission, startling, not to say nauseating, were performed merely to save them a lot of bother. I fancy Johnny Turk had been more free-and-easy in his search parties. . . .

Sometimes we would enter a dwelling to find a crowd of children all looking suspiciously round-cheeked. They were holding papa's ammunition and looking perfectly innocent about it. But the biggest find was in the rafters of an old house, where we discovered the dissembled parts of three machine guns. The householder was promptly taken out and flogged in the open square for all to see.

It is doubtful whether such punishments had any effect upon the

Arabs bent on treachery. We had hardly dug in when Johnny started to throw his shells over, and it was pretty evident that there were many spies in our midst, for he was astonishingly accurate when he made targets of the dwelling used by the headquarters staff, the barracks, and the various dumps. He threw one or two into the hospital, killing men in their beds.

There was only one way the Arabs could get in touch with Johnny, and that was by swimming across the river during the night. We lay on the banks night after night, staring at the water, waiting for the slightest sign of movement. Then, one night, they came, five of them, one after the other, like lambs to slaughter. Two of them slipped into the water with hardly a sound and began to pull with long steady strokes. We let them go a few yards. They were followed by three more, and they were allowed to pass. Then the sergeant of our patrol opened the fire. We followed, taking pot-shots at those dim figures bobbing up and down in the water. There was a yelp, a pair of arms shot up ... another . . . another. . . . Rifles crackled in a rapid volley. Silence. The water was calm, sluggish once more. Five Arab spies had gone home.

Just the same, information continued to leak out to the Turks. We moved quarters more than once. The hospital was shifted. But Johnny kept on finding the vital spots. No one could get out of the town, nor into it, except by swimming the river at dead of night, for there was a double-armed guard the whole way round.

Men, women and children were killed in the streets. Sometimes we were turned out for a spot of stretcher-bearing. Even hardened warriors could sicken at the sight of children with their faces in ribbons, limbs blown off, some of them reduced to bleeding pulp. Their shrieks were heart-rending. Children are children the world over, whatever their creed or race.

Yet the populace had the opportunity to clear out when they knew we were falling back on the town. They elected to stay. Even though they must have realised exactly what it would mean—for they were there when we shelled Johnny Turk out of the place. Certainly they did not expect us to stay so long, nor could they have known what the outcome of that siege must be.

General Townshend issued the following *communiqué* to the troops:

I intend to defend Kut-el-Amarah and not to retire any further. Reinforcements are being sent at once from Basrah to relieve us.

The honour of our mother country and the Empire demands that we all work heart and soul in the defence of this place. We must dig in deep and dig in quickly, and then the enemy's shells will do little damage. We have ample food and ammunition, but commanding officers must husband the ammunition and not throw it away uselessly.

The way you have managed to retire some eighty or ninety miles under the very noses of the Turks is nothing short of splendid, and speaks eloquently for the courage and discipline of this force.

We learned that the relief force was in the country and that it would advance as far as Ali Gharbi, there to be rallied for the great drive through the Turks to Kut. The next news we had was that the relieving force must fight its way towards us, since the Turks were then invading the country in vast numbers. What we thought would be a matter of days was likely to be several weeks, *even months!*

I don't think we worried a great deal in those early days of the siege. We were quite happy to leave all that to the general and his staff. We never doubted that Townshend would get us out. He had organised so many astonishing feats since he came into the country that it never occurred to us that this one would have him beaten.

We settled in for a week or two! Johnny kept us occupied. He had a sufficient force all around us to make us realise that we were completely hemmed in. His firing rarely ceased, night or day. For us there were all manner of fatigue jobs, duty in the trenches, duty in the fort, guarding the dumps, the stores and the river banks.

The enemy's guns had found the old mud fort very early in our stay. He was intent on knocking it to bits. He had been there himself and knew just what it was made of. The more mud bricks the Turks blew into dust the more securely we built it up again with sandbags. And not always sandbags. There was one particularly strenuous engagement when the fort was bombarded for hours on end and we could not get sandbags fast enough. Somebody started bringing up bags of flour! We must have used several hundreds around the walls of the fort. Fools that we were. The day was to come when we should experience terrible need for bread!

But soldiers rarely think of tomorrow. We were being quite well fed. We should not lack water with the river two-thirds way around us. A full tummy and full ammunition pouches—why should we worry? We had been over most of the hovels and houses occupied by the 5,000 householders of Kut and the stunts had brought us much knowledge of this and that secret retreat. In spite of our strenuous duties, we found ways and means of sneaking away, as soldiers always will, mostly during the night, to one or other of our discoveries.

Many days went by before I came upon Latifah, however. But I found her at last. It was the sheerest accident. I was with a detachment at the time, patrolling the *bazaar* quarter. We had broken off for a brief spell. Then the opportunity came for shooting—with camera—an old Arabian woodturner who was working a lathe with his toes. It seemed too good to miss. I shall not soon forget taking that shot. While I was sighting I saw Latifah idling about in the crowd not many yards away. She looked lovelier than ever! And I was scared stiff. I did not show it, however, as I proceeded calmly about getting my picture.

I thought hard. I was on duty. If I rushed over to her—these fellows in the patrol would see me. I was not worrying about a possible wigging from the corporal. Anything that he might do simply left me cold. But I was worrying about this bunch of Tommies. I knew my Tommies. There was hardly a one I'd trust where a pretty girl was concerned! Not in Kut at that date, anyhow. What on earth was I to do? In a moment she would be gone!

I strolled back to the boys, trying to look as if I had not just seen the loveliest creature in Arabia. It was not easy. I am no poker face. All sorts of crazy schemes flashed through my mind in those frantic moments. Throw a fit? Go sick! I never felt so fit in my life! I wanted to jump over the housetops, tear up trees by the roots! But I could not walk up to a girl because a bunch of Tommies might horn in! It was the most exasperating situation. Better miss the chance, thought I, than let these *wallahs* in on anything like this.

Steve was right. I certainly was crazy about that pale-faced Circassian child-woman. For we had tried the Sink several times, and always drew a blank. The den was going as strongly as ever. So far, none of the other boys had discovered the place. We kept the rendezvous a dead secret. "*Never introduce your Dinah to a pal,*" was our slogan.

And then I caught Latifah's eye. She just stared. It was a puzzling look. I could not tell whether she had recognised me or not. She was heavily cloaked, with her face half covered. She turned abruptly and disappeared into the crowd. But, I pondered, she must have recognised me. I was hurt! Incredible, but true! Since she knew me, why did she run away? For the remainder of that afternoon I kept on asking myself footling questions—and all over a Circassian girl!

I sneaked away that night and made my way to the Sink. The place was full. Nobody interfered with me as I passed through the saloon and down the passage to Latifah's room. She was there! I had hardly closed the door when she began—spitting venom like a gutter brat, biting off telling epithets in French, English and her own native *patois*. The onslaught left me gasping. It was hardly the reception I'd anticipated! I saw there was nothing to do but let it boil over.

Oh, yes, she had seen me in the *bazaar*. That was why she had appeared in her old room. She guessed I'd come along. She wanted the opportunity to let off steam. What sort of an honourable Englishman was I? Did I often go around betraying girls who had given me much happiness—reporting them to the police as spies! She was no spy! No spy! She had given me only love! And in return I sent her to the English soldiers' prison! Did I always pay for my pleasures in that way? And so on, *ad nauseum*.

I began to get the drift of her tirade. She was evidently under the impression that I was responsible for the apprehending of the spies who had been shot on that memorable morning. Then she had been working for those agents? And this place had been their secret retreat? It was natural that, since she had been trying to get information from me, she should think I was playing the game of counter-espionage officially.

It took a long time to clear up this confusion of conjectures. And a longer time to convince her that I had played no part in sending her to prison as an associate of enemy spies. I succeeded in the end. When she began to sob as if her heart were breaking I could not make up my mind whether she was just an innocent kid or a darned clever woman. She protested that she had not known her master was a spy against the English, that she was astounded when she learned he had been executed for spying and that she must go to prison for assisting him.

It was even more puzzling to me! I, of course, knew nothing of the case against the spies who were executed that morning. It was not for a common Tommy to inquire into these things, but merely his job to shoot at those whom the authorities call spies. That was the most difficult part of all to explain. Latifah could not understand that I, a British soldier, did not know how and why her master had been convicted and shot—why she had been sent to prison, even though she were finally satisfied that I had had no part in the affair.

Considering all of which, how could I begin to ask why she had always been so persistent in her queries about the Army's movements, whether there were many other soldiers coming into Iraq, and so forth? I decided to leave the matter where it was for the nonce.

She dried the tears and smiled again. The child was born to the art of love-making. She couldn't help it. She was the oddest mixture—devil-cat one minute, angel the next. But the most fascinating creature I've ever met. When I told her that I had been searching for her since we returned to Kut, she laughed.

"But, *mon cheri*, it is only this day I come to Kut!"

"D'you mean, you haven't been in the town until today?"

She nodded.

"But that's impossible! Nobody can get into Kut—or out of it!"

Whereupon she laughed more merrily than ever. The music rolled off her full ripe lips, peal on peal. She was tickled to death!

"I came in this day! I go out this day if I wish!"

"But how? Can you swim the river? And how did you get past the guards? You cannot have come in by the north. There are miles of trenches across."

"I cannot swim the river. I do not come that way—nor through the trenches."

"Then—how?"

She shook her head and laughed again.

"There is a way, *mon cheri*."

I saw she had no intention of telling me—then, for she suddenly became agitated and pressed me not to speak of her coming, not to tell anyone that there was some secret way into Kut. I was satisfied, realising that the knowledge might well be useful later. If there were some way of getting into Kut without the authorities knowing of it—then there was a way out! The sudden realisation of that shook me up quite a lot. I had by no means given up my hair-brained scheme of breaking away from all this. . . .

"But outside of Kut—what is there? Nothing but desert."

"There are villages—especially in the east where the sun comes in the mornings. . . ."

"Yes?" said I, invitingly.

"But it is nothing—a village. When I left the prison I went there to some people I know. They are Christians too . . . Sabians . . . I was happy with them. Then they said the soldiers had come to Kut. I come too."

"Sabians? What are Sabians?"

"You do not know? But Sabians are Christians. You are Christian. I am Christian. Sabians are John Baptist Christians, and they follow the stars."

I did not listen to any more. I realised only that here was a family of Christians in this benighted country who might be helpful one day, and they lived in some remote village near the Persian border. . . . My head was afire. . . . Thoughts raced. . . . I would not whisper of my plans to Latifah then. There was plenty of time, plenty of time. I must think this thing out carefully.

Not a soul must know of my schemes, not even Steve or Cockney Joe. I would work out my own salvation. There was a way out of Kut, a safe way, of which the authorities were ignorant. Across the desert was a family of Christians. I did not know what Sabians were then. Nor did I care. It was sufficient that this friendly family were not Moslems. That fact made them safe in my excited mind. I sneaked back to quarters that night in a daze of heated and excited plottings and schemings, incredibly thrilled by this brainstorm. . . .

Thus young Tiger, still in his 'teens, sick in his soul with the horrors and bestialities of war.

CHAPTER 8

Hell in a Besieged Town

Added to the horrors and bestialities of war was the terrifying prospect of starvation, of starving slowly to death while we kept the Turks at bay and waited and hoped for the advent of the relieving force. The weeks went by, dragging the heavy days on leaden feet. For six weeks we did not even see an aeroplane, nor any other sign that the reinforcements somewhere south were keeping touch. We were just hemmed in. So far as the troops knew, we might live and die in Kut and never again know the world without.

The force was on the defence every minute of every day. The Turks shelled us incessantly. Sometimes we would quieten them with our guns for a short spell. And then again would begin the nerve-wrecking zoom and crash of common shells and shrapnel, spreading hot lead over civilian and soldier alike. Nights were made hideous with the racket of explosions. Tommies got on each other's nerves. Bully beef, Arab black bread—God knows what it contained!—and *char*, was no diet for sick soldiers. There were minor riots in the bazaar and men were "clinked," but I saw no single instance of field punishment number one in Kut, Townshend was a wise general. It was only the troops' faith in the man that kept them going as long as they did.

There were, of course, several desertions. Some got away. Others were potted at in the river until they had to turn back, drenched and more miserable than ever. There were cases, too, of our own men being shot as they attempted to swim the river at dead of night, under the impression that they were Arabs carrying information to the enemy. Heaven alone knows what happened to the Tommies who got away from Kut and into the desert. Maybe some of them managed to trek down river and make contact with the relieving force. But the chances are that the Arabs got them.

There was nothing in the nature of a fortress about Kut. If there had been, things might have been vastly different. The old fort was built of mud bricks, which was all very well for old-fashioned and savage warfare. It was no use against Johnny's shells. We rebuilt it time and time again, strengthened it solidly with sandbags, but always we worked under shell fire, and men went down like ninepins. Trenches, however, well built, must cave in under the blast of perpetual shelling. Ours certainly did time after time.

And once Johnny took advantage of the situation and rushed the trenches. That was on December 10. They pressed our northern front severely for several hours and it seemed to be their intention to break into Kut by way of our entrenched position. We knew that if the gigantic force broke through we were finished. They would simply sweep over us and cut us to bits. Johnny was not allowed to get over, however. We shattered his line with a terrific blast of machine-gun and rifle fire. Johnny was no good in the open. He turned and scattered back to his own trenches. The enemy had lost heavily. The dead and wounded lay thickly about the open desert which stretched between their trenches and ours. They were left to rot in the sun.

Two days later, just at dusk, the enemy made another attempt to storm our trenches. We met them with volley after volley of withering rifle fire. On they came, grey figures massed solidly in a tremendous effort to carry our position. Our machine guns sprayed them with deadly effect. We saw them dropping in their tracks, a ghastly curtain of men thrown at us in a desperate effort to capture our trenches and rush the town. Still they came, massed solidly like a human wall of flesh, into which the stuttering machine guns drilled gaps. . . . It went on most of the night. Sometimes they would come within a few yards of our barbed wire—only to be shot to their knees, yelping and yelling like wounded animals. Never was there such a colossal and blood-thirsty wastage of men. Lives were literally thrown away by the hundred. Many were trapped in the barbed wire entanglements. Many threw away their arms and tumbled headlong into our trenches out of sheer terror.

When dawn came all was quiet once more, except for the piteous cries of the men left out there in the open. They had to stay, and we had to tolerate the sickening moans and cries, for the Turks dared not come out for them. Over two hundred prisoners and deserters fell among us during that ghastly night. They told us that some ten thousand troops had been rushed on the position, and that there were

93

more than two thousand casualties. There were several German officers among them, and they estimated that something like seven thousand rounds of shell had been poured into us in the last twenty-four hours. We lost 120 men killed and wounded.

I stopped one in the left shoulder and was in dock for the next three weeks. But no man stayed in hospital longer than he could possibly help. The building was constantly shelled, and it is no fun to be shot at when you can't reply. Fortunately mine was only a flesh wound. I was back at work in twenty days. Those poor devils in hospital were having a perfectly putrid time. I saw a medical officer, an orderly, patient and bed as well all blown to pieces when that corner of the dock was shot to hell. The very vibration of the shell as it whistled through the air sent us crashing to the ground as if we had actually been hit!

After those insane attempts to rush us, Johnny appeared to give up the idea of direct attack upon the entrenched position, and started in with a serious and unceasing siege bombardment. He kept it up for days, hoping maybe that his persistency would start something among the civilian population. We, however, had the inhabitants well in hand by this time. Our situation was far too desperate to permit the natives any licence whatever. The slightest suspicion of treachery—and the rations were then being carefully doled out to all—and punishment came in swift and certain death. Moreover, we had imprisoned all the *sheiks* and *khans* and headmen of the town, and were holding them as hostages. The population was cowed—where it wasn't sullen and treacherous.

It was known that Arabs were leaving the town by some means. But the way could not be discovered. Johnny Turk was kept informed and we did not know how. I knew there was a secret way out. At all events, I knew that Latifah knew of such a way. I passionately wanted to take this story to the authorities at this time, for I realised that this secret exit was a menace to us all.

But Latifah had disappeared. On the few rare occasions when I could sneak away, I sought her out. She was not to be located in her old haunt. How could I report what I knew when the girl was not there to support my tale? I thought hard at this time. It was not enough to report that there was a secret means of ingress and egress. The town had already been raked from end to end, as I well knew. Just the same, this appalling responsibility weighed heavily with me.

I would debate for hours, as I lounged against the muck of a trench wall, arguing with myself as to whether I should report just all that I knew. I should be "clinked" for having lost track of the source of such information, for not having reported Latifah as soon as I learned of the secret getaway; but that was not worrying me then. I was a bundle of nerves, sick and weary and stupid with the incessant digging and firing and fighting. If I could have come upon the girl during those days of gnawing terror, when we fought ankle-deep in mud and blood, I should have dragged her by the scruff of her lovely neck to the first officer in sight.

I was crazy with malaria and a dirty aching wound that would not heal. But I would not report sick at such a time. There were hundreds of other fellows in just as bad a plight as I . . . I lay in the filth of the trench and groped my way through days of terror. Every bursting shell tore at my vitals, shook me from head to foot, jangling the nerves and hammering at my brain. Hell could hold no worse tortures than these. I got it into my head that I was being repaid for my treachery to my country. This secret locked within me assumed gigantic proportions. It racked my mind during waking hours. I suffered the tortures of the damned in terrorising, fitful sleep.

I knew that men were looking at me queerly—especially Steve. I would catch him eyeing me. I knew what that meant. He thought I couldn't stand the strain, that I was going loopy. He was wrong. It was not the unrelieved strain of trenchwork that was sending me berserk. It was the thought of Latifah and what she knew. Of course, she had gone back to that village. . . . Kut had become too hot for her tender flesh. She had scuttled. And that was that. So much for love. . .

Supposing the Turks arranged with the Arabs who were keeping in touch with them some sort of organised revolt in the town—a revolt timed to coincide with a fresh attack from without! If such a thing happened, I should be responsible. At all events, that was how my warped mentality viewed the situation at that time.

As December advanced, the floods came. Rain poured down in sheets. We were repeatedly washed out of the trenches. We had to organise relays of men to bail out the water, and we waded knee-deep in the filth while we worked. I remember working alongside Steve about this time, when he accidentally came into contact with me as I slithered about in the mud and slush. He grabbed me by the arm.

"Jumping Jupiter! You're as hot as hell, Tiger! Why don't you report sick and get into dock out of this blasted muck!"

"I'm all right. Nice and cool in the water."

"Don't be a blasted fool! You get out o' this, you little sap!"

"And you mind your own damned business!"

"Huh? Listen, kid. You can't muck about with a temperature like you've got. You'll konk out. I thought you was jest going crazy with the strain of this business. But it's the malaria. Get out of here before it gets you down for good an' all."

I was carried out eventually. Steve told me later that I was raving like a lunatic. I was not surprised. But even more interesting was the story told me by the R.A.M.C. orderly when, after several days, I got on my feet again. He seemed to have been terribly amused by my delirious gabblings—about a beautiful girl who knew a secret way out of Kut, whom I knew, and whom I had failed to report to the authorities!

"Malaria often takes a fellow like that," said he, sympathetically. "Don't worry, that's the main thing. You have been worrying about our ever getting out of Kut again. I can tell that by the nature of your delirium. Don't do it. We'll get out, all right. S'long, chum. Watch your temperature now."

I went back to work, thinking how ridiculously my ravings had been construed. It was Christmas Eve. I spent it in helping to defend the old fort. There was nothing to mark that Christian date. It didn't mean anything to Johnny Turk. It wasn't even December 24 to him. It was just another occasion for a frightful bombardment. I had arrived in time for another of those persistent shell blastings that seemed to shake the earth. Johnny made huge breaches in our first wall of defence that night. He was doing his damndest to shell his way into the fort. By midnight we were forced to retire to our second wall of defence. Which meant that Johnny was in possession of the first line.

Naturally his big guns ceased then, for he was afraid of hitting his own men. We charged back to the front line, filling the walled trench with bombs as we ran. There was a short, swift, hand-to-hand scuffle with butt and bayonet, and Johnny was dislodged. Not many of them got away again. The trench was filled with dead and wounded. They were tossed over the barbed wire entanglements. This was no occasion for the niceties of civilised warfare. We had to defend ourselves against another attack. We could not do it efficiently with the stench of reeking bodies under our feet. There are two things in this world that always smell—cabbages and Turks.

Christmas Day dawned and Johnny kept on sending his presents. It was his ironic idea of celebrating the birth of the Prophet—our prophet, not the Moslems'. At least, the day was warm and sunny.

There is no winter in Iraq, nothing to mark the Christmas season except rain, and not always that. When the shell fire died down later in the morning we could hear the enemy *digging!* They had come up under the bombardment and dug in. Johnny is a wonderful excavator! He is second brother to the mole. He had dug in, under our very noses, less than eighty yards away!

Orders were given for his removal. He could not be allowed to come so close—not on Christmas Day, anyway. We went over the top, leapt the wire, and yelled our way towards his new trenches. In a few moments there was the hideous spectacle of two opposing forces of men throwing bombs at each other at about twelve yards distant. How can I ever forget Christmas Day, 1915? The day we threw puddings full of powder at each other! But the Turk was true to his pet aversion about fighting in the open. His new trenches gave him little or no protection. So he turned and bolted, leaving bloody losses behind. His assaulting columns away behind him dared not come up, and we had to scuttle back, because our artillery boys started throwing a curtain of howitzer fire over us.

After that they gave us a little peace while we got busy retrenching around the old fort and piling up sandbags afresh. In late afternoon we were made aware of the fact that some of the enemy had crawled out to those new earthworks again, for now the place was being used as a sniping post. We learned later from several prisoners that the snipers had spent most of the day in creeping over the ground and pushing dead bodies before them as they progressed. In this way they actually reached the new earthworks not more than eighty yards away, and then started to snipe us.

It is common military practice to oust snipers without delay. Such crack shots can account for many men if they are left any length of time. We let them carry on until darkness descended. Then a party of us, ten in all, crept over the wire and started crawling on our bellies towards the sniping post. We moved slowly, inching our way alligator fashion through a litter of bodies and shell fragments, hardly daring to breathe lest we be picked off and the whole stunt ruined.

It was a night without moon, black as the pit, so that we could hardly see a yard ahead. Grim, still shapes lay about. We never knew from one minute to another that one of these bodies might not become a live sniper. It was a creepy, eerie jaunt. Faint sounds came to us on the dead night air. Once I hit up against a dead Turk and recoiled. I must have spat disgustedly. The sergeant lay flat on his tummy and shook his fist at me. We lay as flat as the landscape for several agonising moments and listened with strained ears.

The N.C.O. raised himself a couple of inches or so and started to crawl forward again. We followed. The things men will do! Slowly, by infinitesimal degrees, we drew nearer our objective. We must have spent the better part of an hour making those few yards. It seemed that we should never be done. Our N.C.O. must have been a contortionist. He would take an age over a couple of yards, his long slim body hardly raised from the ground, then rest gently down, while the strain was taken from aching muscles and we regained our breath. I thought we should never make it without those devils at the sniping post hearing us. We should make lovely targets if they heard us and raised themselves above those earthworks. It was ghastly to realise that one was in No Man's Land and within a few yards of six or seven crack shots. . . .

We were on top of those heaps of earth and rubble before we realised the fact. Suddenly the sergeant straightened up, paused, stared round on the dim holes a yard or two away. We had grown accustomed to the darkness by this time. The outline of those new entrenchments was clear enough for us to see. But not a sound came from them! Had we come on a fool's errand? Could it be that Johnny had fallen back on his front line? Were the snipers gone?

Something of the sort must have been in the N.C.O.'s mind.

"Come on!" he snapped, not troubling to whisper.

We went in a bunch, made a hell dive for those holes. The snipers were asleep. Whoever they had left on guard must have slept too. We wakened them with fast-discolouring bayonets. They were never sufficiently awake to put up any resistance. They woke to be stabbed to death. A series of startled yelps, then grunts, dying gurgles. In under five minutes the place was made to resemble a slaughter house. Hardly a sound got beyond those half-dug trenches. We climbed out of the holes, kicking clods of earth on to the still-warm bodies as we left. Thereafter a doubled-up race back to the fort.

"All right," growled the sergeant, as he went off to his own dugout. "You fellows had better try and get some shut-eye. Don't think we shall be worried with snipers tonight. Well done, lads!"

CHAPTER 9

Foretaste of Famine

Nineteen Hundred and Sixteen! The old year went and the new came in, but it made no difference to our position at Kut. It was still, as some wag remarked, nineteen hundred and wartime. There was an incident at the old fort on New Year's Day of the kind that was becoming a trifle too common among the Indian troops. A *sepoy* on sentry suddenly turned about, fired a couple of shots at an officer, and then ran for the Turkish lines. He was caught before he could get many yards away, tried by court martial and shot. There was quite a number of *sepoys* deserting to the enemy at this time. The rats had an idea that the ship was sinking so they scuttled. There was a lot of self-mutilation too, trigger fingers being shot off to avoid further service.

It was true that I, too, wished to get away from the miseries and horrors of Kut. But the dose of malaria must have altered my views as to what I should do if ever I found that secret way out. Certainly I should not go over to Johnny. I am no Moslem! My plan then was to get down country somehow and link up with the relief force. Men were still getting away. Maybe they had found the way out. Whether they got across the border to Persia or down to the reinforcements was more than we knew.

Another disquieting fact at this time was the sight of new Turkish divisions marching down the left bank of the Tigris towards our relieving forces. We could see them from the top of the fort, column after column, miles of men and guns and transport. We of the fort garrison knew then that it must take some time before we could be relieved, since it must mean heavy engagements to drive back these great columns of fresh troops. One column was estimated to be five miles in length and containing 8,000 men with guns and squadrons of cavalry.

We looked at each other then, as men will when such disheartening sights cannot be denied, and we wondered if we should *ever* get out of Kut.

"If the Indian Government have been as niggardly about the numbers for the relief force as they were about the original expeditionary force—well, I guess we ain't got a chance in hell!"

I had never heard Steve talk in that fashion before.

"Steve, if you knew of a safe way out of Kut . . . what would you do?"

"Don't be a sap, Tiger. There ain't no safe way out. You've seen what happened to those other fellows!"

"To some of them—yes. Not all. But supposing we were to discover some perfectly safe way out, some secret way not known to Divisional Headquarters . . . what then?"

"Say, Tiger! You suggesting we should desert?"

"No. I'm suggesting that if we could find a way out, we should take a chance."

"Huh? Supposing we did find this secret way out—though it sounds like a dime adventure yarn to me—well, where'n hell could we go?"

"I suppose you'll agree that some of the boys got away safely?"

"I doubt it, old fellah, I doubt it. An' what I'd like to know is where they went, even if they did get away?"

"There are only two routes a Britisher would take—either across to the Persian border or downstream to link up with the relief force."

"In either event a fellah would be caught by the brown boys out there and handed over to the women—so the dames could play tit-tat-too on a white man's tummy. Guess I'd sooner starve to death!"

"We look like doing that before long."

"What's bitten you, Tiger?"

"Well, we're on half rations now. You've seen what the relief force must break through before they can reach us! I'm damned if I like the idea of hanging on here while Johnny keeps us hemmed in with his shells till our rations run out. . . ."

"That idea doesn't appeal to me either, old fellah. It's a hell of a prospect. But that crazy alternative o' yours is worse. An' the river's in flood, an' I'm no great shakes at swimming, an' I hate being shot at when I can't pot back . . . an'—aw, hell! Lay off, for the love of Mike!"

"Listen, Steve. I'm not such a crass idiot as you seem to think.

Swimming the river never entered my head. There is a way out. . . ."

"Huh! D'ya mean a secret way out of Kut?"

"Yes."

"All right, kid. Spill it. I guess I'll buy this one!"

"I'm serious, Steve. You remember Latifah?"

"What! That bitch again!"

"Bitch or no bitch, she came into Kut weeks after we took over, and she's disappeared—which means she has got out again. . . ."

"Did she tell you about this way out?"

Steve gave that peculiar lift of his bushy eyebrows so characteristic of him when more than usually interested. I explained how I found Latifah and what her visit had revealed.

"Say, Tiger. I'm just an American guy enjoying myself around these parts, but I guess if any dame had come to me with a yarn like that, I'd have picked her up and handed her over to G.H.Q."

"Not if you felt as I did at that time. In any case, I don't believe you would do that with a woman—not a white woman."

"Maybe you're right. But I should have got the story out of her some ways. . . ."

"Don't you see! That was my intention. The next I knew she'd flown!"

"You've tried the Sink?"

"Heavens! It's a wonder I haven't been clinked—the number of times I've been and sneaked off to that place!"

"Well, Tiger, there don't appear to be anythin' you can do till she rolls up again, huh?"

"Me? Meaning you wouldn't?"

"All right, kid. Supposing she does, an' supposing she's ready to show us this secret passage or whatever the ten-cent racket—is what have you?"

"At best, the opportunity to get out of Kut and make contact with the relieving force, tell 'em the true state of affairs in Kut—which they don't seem to appreciate—and tell 'em, too, about this way into the town. They might be able to make use of such information, you know!"

"Ain't you got this all wrong, kid? Supposing she turns up and gives us this information, couldn't it be used by G.H.Q. in Kut? Maybe as a way out?"

"Steve, I've thought of this thing for many weeks and from every possible angle. The point is that if Latifah knows of such a thing, there's quite a number of Arabs in this town who know of it too. If, in the last resort, headquarters decided to use this as a way out of Kut, rather than have the men starve to death, isn't it likely that the spies would know and give the game away to Johnny. I know nothing about it, but it is possible that the way is not one that could accommodate troops marching four abreast in vast numbers, much less the necessary transport that must move with them, if they are not to starve to death as soon as they get outside. I don't see how G.H.Q. could make use of it, even if they knew of its existence."

"Sure they could! They could put a guard on it and nobble every Arab that tried to make his getaway."

"All right. If we find it, what's wrong with making our exit and leaving a message behind explaining how we got out?"

"Sounds loopy to me, Tiger. But I guess we can decide what to do when we find the darned passage or whatever it is." [1]

So, for the time being, we had to leave it at that. Days were to come when we longed to find out that secret, when we should not hesitate for a moment to use *any way out!* The longer we stayed in Kut the more securely the enemy was able to entrench around us. Our engineers estimated that there must have been between thirty and forty miles of earthworks around us. As each day passed, our chances of breaking out became more and more remote. We were trapped like rats, and there came the day when we were made horribly aware of the fact.

As the January days advanced we had one or two rare visits from the air force—such as it was! They dropped weighted packages into the town, which were immediately taken to headquarters. We expected to hear of the relief force as a result of these aerial visits. But nothing happened. Apparently there was nothing to report, no cheering news that the long-awaited relief was drawing nearer to the besieged town of Kut. We continued with a monotony of days spent in a fighting defence. Weary men were angered beyond belief at the dearth of news. Demoralisation was growing among the troops. We had then been shut in the town for two months and seemingly the relief force was not big enough or good enough to clear Johnny Turk out of its path and advance to our assistance. What indeed were tired Tommies

---

1. It is not suggested that this is the actual wording of a discussion between Steve Barry and myself. For such passages, one can rely only on memory and diary notes. The importance of the move we eventually made and which grew out of this conversation is justification enough for its reproduction here.

to think?

There occurred at this stage an incident that has never ceased to puzzle me. General Von der Goltz, the German commander-in-chief of the Turkish force, was spotted while paying a visit with his staff to the trenches opposite the old fort. Immediately our artillery opened fire upon him and he had to clear out pretty quickly. Nothing would have pleased the boys more at that time than to have been able to make a direct hit upon the trench he was inspecting. But the general escaped. That was not all. When it was learned at our Divisional Headquarters that an attempt had been made to blow the Turkish army's commander-in-chief to hell, there was a terrific hullabaloo. Inquiries were set afoot as to why such a thing had been done, who had dared to give such an order, who had been responsible for throwing shells in the immediate vicinity of the German general commanding the enemy forces! Apparently the general officer commanding an army is not cannon fodder!

At the end of January a *communiqué* was issued to the troops:

The Relief Force under General Aylmer has been unsuccessful in its efforts to dislodge the Turks entrenched on the left bank of the river, some fourteen miles below the position at Essinn, where we defeated the Turks in September last, *when their strength was greater than it is now*. Our relieving force suffered severe loss and had very bad weather to contend against. They are entrenched close to the Turkish position. More reinforcements are on their way up river and I confidently expect to be relieved some day during the first half of the month of February.

The italics are mine. Here is something else that has never ceased to puzzle me. How could the strength of the Turks be greater in September last than it was at the time of this message? How reconcile this statement with the fact that we had seen many miles of Turkish columns passing down the river bank an its way south to meet the relief force? On the other hand, if the strength of the Turks were greater when we licked them with our puny force in September past, how was it that our reinforcements could not vanquish the Turkish force opposing them now? There could be only one answer to that question. The relief force must be poor in quality and quantity. Once more the Indian Government had failed us. They would not or could not appreciate the true position in Mesopotamia. After fifteen or sixteen months of this campaign, they still did not know how to run it,

The Bridge of Boats across the Tigris at Baghdad

they still thought in brigades when they should have talked in divisions. Clearly, the Indian Government was incapable of controlling the campaign in Mesopotamia. If anyone were responsible for that terrible fiasco, that frightful wastage of human life in slaughter and starvation, that siege *and surrender* of Kut, it was the War Office in India.

True, the conditions in the country were far worse now than they were in September. The rain poured down incessantly. The banks of the rivers overflowed, inundating the country all around. Did we not know that? We were continually washed out of our trenches. We had to work knee-deep in water and filth. We would get the earthworks clear. There would be days when the sun shone. Then we laboured like coolies to reconstruct our entrenchments. And again would come those torrential downpours! Once more we should be flooded out.

The swollen Tigris came up and over, flooding our trenches—first and second lines. The troops had no option but to fall back on the reserve positions and this entirely apart from any enemy action! This caused the old fort to be absolutely isolated and without protection. We were engaged night and day, standing up to our knees in mud and slush, in fighting the floods which at one period threatened to wash us out of Kut altogether. If Johnny could have advanced at that time—by means of rafts and *bellums* such as we had used soon after landing in the country—he could have blown us to bits, for we were singularly helpless against those dreaded Tigris floods.

Instead of which, we contrived to take advantage of the flooded state of *his* trenches to take it out of him—at least, our gunnery boys did. I am convinced that whatever else we lacked, we certainly did have the finest artillery soldiers in that country. When the floods caused the Turks to flee from their front line trenches and race across the open to their reserve positions, our gunners opened fire and peppered them severely. Hundreds of them never reached the safety of the reserves. Bits and pieces of them were seen floating on the water for days, until the waters subsided in fact; and the stench from those sodden and putrefying bodies when the sun did come out and get to work upon them was appalling. The effluvium got into one's nostrils, sickening the senses, tainting one's food, turning the stomach.

Those trenches were more suitable for canal bargees than soldiers. But even so, no sort of flood had stayed our advance in those early days of landing in the country. We had used three hundred *bellums* and other craft, armoured with machine-gun shields, in the great drive around Kurnah. We had to contend with a river that had overflowed its banks for miles. The villages, I well remember, that stood on higher ground, had looked like so many little islands in a great expanse of ocean. Yet *we* advanced! What was the matter with this relief force that stayed put because of floods? That was the sort of question we of the old guard asked ourselves, even while we fought with the flooded entrenchments that threatened to finish us altogether.

The next phase came when the tinned bully gave out and we started to kill our horses and mules for meat. That was serious enough—not because we disliked the taste of horseflesh. When horseflesh is the only meat, one eats and that is all there is to it. But there must still have been some twelve thousand troops in Kut, and some five thousand Arabians, most of whom were fed by our soup kitchens. How long would a few hundred horses last us? All vegetables gave out. Scurvy and other horrible skin diseases came in. The Arab populace became more truculent as the rations were more scantily doled out. But the feeling of the troops was that the soansos were damned lucky to get anything to eat at all.

By this time the *bazaar* quarter was bankrupt. Crude wooden shutters were nailed over what had once been food, vegetable and fruit stalls. More search parties were turned out. We were not looking for arms this time. We searched for secret stores of food. We found a few. They were mostly hidden beneath the floors of the more well-to-do Arabian dwellings. We came upon stores of wheat, dates, vegetables and fruit.

In one house we discovered hundreds of cans of jam, bully-beef and cheese! It was all regular army issue and had obviously been stolen in the early days of the siege. The cans were packed tightly in between the rafters of the roof and then boarded over! It was this unusual style of boarding between the rafters that had first attracted the attention of the sergeant of our party. He ordered one of the men to get busy on the boards with his entrenching tools—just in case there might be something behind. A couple of boards were wrenched off and the little square cans came tumbling down at our feet.

I shall not forget that scene in a hurry. We were too astonished to do anything but stare at these luxuries for several seconds, we who were trying to exist on everlasting and nauseating doses of horse-flesh stew! The old Arab owner of the dwelling stood by the wall of the room, his hands working and his grey-bearded face twitching. His two women folk crouched beside him. The eyes of the men in our party—there were eight of us—turned on the abject trio. That brown ancient and his two young *paramours* knew their hour had come. I could see death in their eyes. You can't steal good food from half-starved soldiers and get away with it.

This was no case for headquarters. We all agreed on that without a word being spoken. The sergeant walked slowly over to the Arab, grabbed him by the cloth-stuff of his chest and backside, and heaved him into the further corner of the room. One heard the sickening crack. His head was knocked in. He needed no further attention.

The shrieks and screams of the women availed them nothing. Infuriated men wasted no time. Rifles rattled in a ragged volley. The bodies were chucked into the dirty alley. Then we set to work to remove the remainder of the boards and retrieve our rations of jam and bully-beef and cheese!

CHAPTER 10

The Starving Garrison

During the month of February, 1916, we were harassed to death by repeated night and day attacks. On the starvation diet we were fast becoming physical wrecks. Famine stared us in the face and we couldn't do a thing about it. All over the place men were dropping like rotten sheep with disease. There was not a physically fit man in the town of Kut. We were being ravaged by a queer, gnawing hunger that horse and black bread in no way appeased—and by every sort of dirty fever, by cholera, small-pox, dysentery, boils, beastly skin eruptions. We were shot at from within and from without.

We had, too, the spectacle of skinny and emaciated children walking around the streets, mere bundles of bones wrapped in rags, pleading piteously for grub. Mothers, terror walking their brains and looking out of their soft, black eyes, bared their breasts and showed us dry, empty, sagging paps. We could sit over our miserable meals and talk about "poor old so-an-so" having "gone west," without caring very much as to who would be next. One might as well be kicked to death as starved to death and be shot at in the bargain.

It left us cold to learn that the relief force was slow in coming to our aid because of the lack of adequate transport. We knew all about that. And look how we had travelled! General Aylmer should realise that he was in the Indian Army. Transport indeed! Our view was that "Townshend would have done it!" Pity he could not have been taken out of Kut and down the line to that snail-pace force. He'd have brought 'em up quickly enough!

It was during this month that a German monoplane came over the town and started to drop bombs all over the place. He did not do a lot of damage—except to still further shatter our *morale*. We took machine guns up on the house-tops and scared him off. If we could have brought him down he would have been torn limb from limb. We had trouble enough without having to put up with this new war from the air. We sent a pelting hail of lead in his direction. He waved his hand and passed on.

We watched the Battle of Hannah from the roofs. This was one of the desperate attempts to get near us. Though the engagement must have been more than twenty miles away, we could actually see belching smoke. Shells were bursting with the clearness of a photographer's magnesium flash. We could hear the distant thunder of heavy guns. We almost began to hope. It looked as if something were really happening this time. We watched for hours, hoping against hope to see the black smudge come up over the skyline . . . any old thing that would mark the retreat of the Turkish divisions. But it never came. The battle of Hannah was another washout. Johnny was not to be dislodged by any slim body of British relief.

In addition to keeping the relief at bay, Johnny was able also to reinforce his positions all round Kut. Up to March 1st we had 2,930 casualties and on that day the enemy opened another of his blasting bombardments. We learned that he had twenty-one guns in action. He filled the town with shrapnel and lyddite, blew up houses and scattered the inhabitants to hell. One or two alleys were positively littered with bleeding limbs . . . men, women and children lay about in the grim shapes of death . . . a child flat on its tummy with arms outspread . . . a woman crumpled up in death with a live baby under her . . . youngsters who had run hand-in-hand in terror left evidences in death of that terror. . . .

Three German monoplanes came over and dropped about fifty bombs—most of them on the hospital, a converted bazaar, where the Red Cross Flag flew—killing sick and wounded as they lay in their beds. We pelted them with machine guns from the roofs, but never a hit was registered. Such improvised anti-aircraft guns were of little use, for the aircraft appeared to pass back and forth over the town as they pleased. Johnny was doing his damndest to break down our defence, which he knew must be sadly weakened by this time. It was the worst onslaught we had had thus far. And yet, there was still room for Tommy's ironic humour. One heard him singing:

When this bloody war is over,
Oh, how happy we shall be!

To the tune of a once-popular hymn!

Maybe the terrific bombardment was Johnny's answer to the punishment our relief force had given his troops at Hannah. In the second week of March another big battle was fought in an endeavour to drive the Turks back. A thick haze lay over the land and we could see but little of what was happening, though we heard the reassuring thunder of guns and knew someone was trying! Moreover, for the first time we stood by, that is, those of us who could still stand, to break out of Kut by means of our one remaining steamer and a few Arab sailing boats, the object being to slaughter the Turks as soon as they hove in sight and thus join up with the advancing relief force. Only the force didn't advance. We listened to their efforts for two days. Another attempt had failed.

It was at this period that General Townshend received a communication from Khalil Pacha, Commanding the Turkish forces in Iraq, which he has since published to the world:

> Your Excellency,   10. 3. 1916.
> The English forces which came to relieve you were compelled to retreat after giving battle at Felahieh and suffering 7,000 casualties.
> After this retreat, General Aylmer, who was a month and a half in making his preparations, yesterday, when he thought he was strong enough, resumed the offensive with the 5th, 6th, 8th and 12th brigades of infantry and one cavalry brigade on the right bank of the Tigris, as you saw. But he was again compelled to retreat, with 4,000 casualties, and I am left with adequate forces.
> For your part, you have heroically fulfilled your military duty. From henceforth I see no likelihood that you will be relieved. According to your deserters, I believe that you are without food and that diseases are prevalent among your troops.
> You are free to continue your resistance at Kut, or to surrender to my forces, which are growing larger and larger.
> Receive, general, the assurances of our highest consideration.
>   Khalil,
>   Commander Turkish Forces in Iraq,
>   Governor of Baghdad.

It is a pity that General Townshend did not inform his troops of this communication at the time—so that they too might laugh. I can assure him or any other general that it is just the sort of thing to hearten troops. I can well imagine what those fellows in Kut would have said in answer to such a message—though I must not write it here! Sick, weary and war-worn as they were, the effect of such colossal effrontery would have caused them to tighten their belts, would have brought a glint of fire into their tired eyes, would have roused their fighting spirit, that spirit expressed in their own words—"Stick it, Tommy! The first ten years is always the worst!"

Instead of which, they were left to ponder upon the repeated failures of the relief force to break through the Turkish lines. The general depression increased. Though we had not entirely lost hope, even then, that act of standing-by in vain gave us a nasty jolt. Maybe we were too weak to put up much resistance against the gloom of pessimism. Also, another batch of Indians took it into their heads to practise self-mutilation at this time, and another bunch of them deserted to the enemy. It was on the cards that Johnny would now give us another walloping. He did. But why repeat the frightful tale of blood and mud and death?

The position then was—a river at flood on three sides of us, on the fourth a flooded area between the Turks' entrenchments and our own, bombs from the air and shells shot at us from every angle of the compass, thousands of Arabs among us who openly sneered at the defenders of a lost cause, disease rampant, a graveyard that grew fatter and fatter—and we were down to our last few horses. . . .

"We couldn't break out now, if we wanted to!" snapped Steve. "That darned river is travelling at about eight knots!"

"Disguised as Arabs, we could get away, even now."

"Supposing that dame of yours was to turn up and show us the way!"

"Suppose you'd take the way out now?"

"Betcha sweet life I would, Tiger. There ain't no point in sticking around here anymore. Johnny has us licked, I guess. We're dying feet upwards . . . but we won't lie down. Gosh! The British Tommy's got sand! I'll say that for him."

We were on the flat roof of a house, squatting under a tarpaulin with a machine gun. We sat and stared at the rain, coming straight down in sheets. I shall never forget it. Never in my life have I felt so miserable. If I hadn't been a soldier I should have wept. Our agony had then been stretched over four months. No man, however much of a stoic he may be, can face such a slow death unmoved. I could understand those Indian *wallahs*. But we were white men backed by military traditions. We were supposed to put up a different front in face of creeping death. We'd got sand! I wondered. It seemed to me it required some courage to shoot off one's own trigger finger or make a sudden dash across that flooded swamp to the enemy's lines.

I think the troops remained staunch because there was nothing else a white man could do. But a great many of them would have cleared out if they could have found a way—other than deserting to the enemy. That, of course, was unthinkable in any event. Sometimes a white man would get to the end of his tether length—and then suicide. But to me, even then and with all we had gone through, life still seemed worthwhile.

Self-preservation is an instinct that reaches deep down. Despite tradition, training, discipline and everything else, there comes a time when a man considers only self. *Dieu et mon droit*, the inscription that figures on badges and equipment of the British Army, was often humorously interpreted by Tommy to mean—"Damn you, Jack, I'm all right." It ceased to be a humorous interpretation in those latter days of the siege of Kut. Men grabbed when and what they could because the conditions were driving them insane.

There were some cases where the men took the law into their own hands, flogging unmercifully those fellows caught in the act of stealing another man's rations. I shudder now at the recollection of one instance. The man had been caught on three or four occasions, but it appeared that no amount of flogging would cure him. I am quite certain he was mad. He was a danger to us all, for I knew how near we could come to emulating him, and that would have been the end. . . . He was reported at last and put away for a spell.

The poor devil came out of prison hungrier than ever! Everyone knew that we were very nearly at the end of our grain. Soon there would be nothing but horses and donkeys. (The Arabs were already eating their donkeys.) But it became a mania with the loopy one to steal bread. He just couldn't leave it alone. He was found early one morning by a patrol near the brick kilns, nailed to a wagon, a gibbering idiot.

I don't think any of us were quite normal in those days.

What would you? We were being shot to death, starved to death, scared to death. Men were dying of horrible and disfiguring diseases. Tetanus, that arched a man's back in the last agonising death throes, claimed many victims as a result of the town's accumulating filth. Dysentery would bring down a whole company at once. Fevers spread because medical and anti-bacterial supplies were giving out. Sentries fainted at their posts. How could men remain sane in such abnormal conditions?

About the middle of March a message from Sir Percy Lake, who had superseded Sir John Nixon as Commander-in-Chief in Iraq, to General Townshend, was issued as a *communiqué* to the troops:

> I can realise to the full, and sympathise most deeply with, the disappointment which both you and your command must feel at our recent failure to relieve you. Rest assured, however, that we shall not abandon the effort, and that for the next attempt the maximum force will be employed.

The commander was wrong. No man could "realise to the full," unless he were in it.

Before March went out, General Gorringe had superseded General Aylmer as Commander of the Relief Force There did not appear to be much confidence in the higher command. Half the Expeditionary Force "D" had gone west. Iraq was becoming a graveyard. Generals were being sacked. It was also a graveyard of reputations. Men and officers of an inadequate relief force were giving their lives in thousands. In Kut we continued to hang on, as Tommy said, "by the skin of our teeth."

The general's *communiqués* became more frequent and more frank:

> I am speaking to you as I did before, straight from the heart, and, as I say, I ask your sympathy for my feelings, having promised you relief on certain dates on the promise of those ordered to relieve us. Not their fault, no doubt—do not think that I blame them. They are giving their lives freely, and deserve our gratitude and admiration. I want you to help me again as before . . . I have had to reduce your ration. It is necessary to do this in order to keep the Flag flying. I am determined to hold out, and I know you are with me in this heart and soul.

Strong picquets were turned out to search the native quarters once again. There had been rumours of cannibalism. We could find no evidence of the sort. But everywhere we went we found men, women and children emaciated beyond belief. Apparently a diet of donkey is not very nourishing. Women and children remained in their beds because they had become too weak to stand. They presented the most sickening sights. Huddled bones in dirty blankets. This, I saw, was the real meaning of the term "beleaguered town." The siege of Ladysmith in the Transvaal War lasted one hundred and twenty days. We had already beaten that record and we looked like doubling it.

(And yet, so strong has been the hush-hush policy regarding Kut at this stage of the Mesopotamian Campaign, that the Siege of Ladysmith in 1899 is more readily recalled than the Siege of Kut in 1915-16!)

The native quarter looked like a city stricken with plague—as indeed it was, for there can be no plague so ghastly as famine. Some of the women and children dragged at our coats, begging for bread, until they had to be beaten off. We were in no case to respond to their pleadings. It was fairly clear, however, that there could be no further discoveries of secret hoards of food. One little episode of that search sticks in the mind. We noticed that some of the Arabs still had tobacco. A detachment of us were passing along a street where a number of Arabs sat cross-legged on a high wooden bench. As we drew level one of the natives, a grey-bearded veteran, took out a cigarette. He was in the act of lighting it when a Tommy dashed towards him and snatched it.

The rest of us eyed that Tommy hungrily while he smoked that cigarette . . . sniffing the smoke. . . . When he threw down the fag-end there was an unholy scramble for it!

About the middle of April a *communiqué* was issued that showed clearly how near the end we were:

> The result of the attack of the Relief Force on the Turks entrenched in the Sannaiyat position is that the Relief has not yet won its way through, but is entrenched close up to the Turks, in places some two to three hundred yards distant. General Gorringe wired me last night that he was consolidating his position as close to the enemy's trenches as he can get, with the intention of attacking again. He had had some difficulty with the flood, which he has remedied.
>
> I have no other details. However, you will see that I must not run any risk over the date calculated to which our rations would last—namely 15th April. As you will understand well, digging means delay, though General Gorringe does not say so.
>
> I am compelled therefore to appeal to you all to make a determined effort to eke out our scanty means so that I can hold out for certain till our comrades arrive, and I know I shall not appeal to you in vain.
>
> I have then to reduce our rations to five ounces of meal for all

ranks, British and Indian.

In this way I can hold out to 21st April, if it becomes necessary, and it is my duty to take all precautions in my power.

I am very sorry I can no longer favour the Indian soldiers in the matter of meal, but there is no possibility of doing so now. It must be remembered that there is plenty of horseflesh which they have been authorised by their religious leaders to eat, and I have to recall with sorrow that by not having taken advantage of this wise and just dispensation, they have weakened my power of resistance by one month.

In my *communiqué* to you of 26th January, I told you that our duty stood out plain and simple; it was to stand here and hold up the Turkish advance on the Tigris, working heart and soul together. I expressed the hope that we would make this defence to be remembered in history as a glorious one and I asked you in this connection to remember the defence of Plevna, which was longer than even that of Ladysmith.

Well! You have nobly carried out your mission; you have nobly answered the trust and appeal I made to you. The whole British Empire, let me tell you, is ringing now with our defence of Kut.

You will all be proud to say one day: 'I was one of the garrison at Kut!' As for Plevna and Ladysmith, we have outlasted them also. Whatever happens now, we have all done our duty. As I said in my report of the defence of this place, which has now been telegraphed to Headquarters—I said that it was not possible in despatches to mention everyone, but I could safely say that every individual in this force had done his duty to his King and Country. I was absolutely calm and confident, as I told you on 26th January, of the ultimate result; and I am confident now. I ask you all, comrades of all ranks, British and Indian, to help me now in this food question in the manner I have mentioned.

Charles Townshend,
Major-General.

Kut-el-Amarah,
10th April, 1916.

At that time many of the Indians sickened and died. For religious reasons they could not, or would not, eat horse. The Indian is more easily dejected than the white man. In such circumstances the strain on him was terrific, added to which was the fact that many of them simply could not eat horse. They died for their religious principles. By April they were dying at the rate of ten a day. Soon Britishers were dying off too, not because they could not eat horse, but because that diet, coupled with the long-drawn-out strain of the past four months, was more than they could bear.

And now we were making "examples" of attempts at desertion to the enemy by Indians who were caught in the act. Their skinny bodies were hanging by the neck, swaying in the breeze, for all men to see.

A great deal of this resulted from Turkish propaganda. Johnny had found some way of getting across No Man's Land at dead of night and depositing bunches of leaflets in the trenches occupied by the Indians. These enjoined the Indian Moslems to break away from the starving British and come over to their brother Moslems the Turks. Johnny went so far as to promise his Indian brother a piece of land and wives. . . .

This had to be stopped. Men were detailed to go over the wire into No Man's Land, there to wait and watch for the arrival of Johnny with more seditious literature. I have heard men talk of the nerve-wracking horrors of the listening posts in Flanders, but they could hardly have been worse than those we experienced in the mud that lay beyond our trenches at Kut.

We lay in the dirt for hours, night after night, waiting and listening, and nothing happened. It was almost impossible to keep awake! Fighting against sleepiness that would creep over one, dulling the senses even while one realised the danger of succumbing, cramping muscles that must be ever on the alert, was an agony I find too difficult to describe. I recall lying behind a heap of dirt with a Gurkha—one of India's finest and toughest warriors—when the dread sleepiness came over me. I begged the little fellow to dig me awake if I should fall off.

I fell asleep. I must have slept three or four hours while that little fellow had kept the post himself! I was suddenly awakened by feeling the Gurkha's hand over my mouth. He was afraid I might shout as I awoke. It took me several seconds to gather my wits. My companion grinned, pointed. I stared into the dimness. Sleep had put a strain on my eyes and it was some time before I could make out the figure of Johnny creeping along on his belly towards us. He was inching his way at such a slow pace that he hardly seemed to move at all.

Gradually he drew nearer, staring not at us but straight at our barbed wire. A bundle hung from his neck—the leaflets, no doubt. I saw that my companion had drawn his knife. He held it ready to strike, but with the blade buried in the dirt so as not to show! This was disastrous, I thought, in a muddled sort of way. I knew the Gurkha would strike to kill as soon as he got his chance. There was every indication that he was going to kill. He was poised for the leap. I dared not utter a word then, dared not tell my companion that we had orders to take Johnny back alive. It was too late. The slightest sound would have ruined everything! Of course, the Gurkha knew as well as I what the orders were. It was just that he had conveniently forgotten!

He leapt suddenly, landing on the back of the crouching figure, simultaneously burying his knife into the back of Johnny's neck, A throaty grunt and the fellow was dead.

"You've finished him! Now there'll be hell to pay! You knew we had to take him in for questioning."

"He is dirty swine, *Sahib*" grinned the Gurkha. "Him bring lies to Moslem *wallahs* and make 'em desert."

"The orders were to take him in alive!"

"*Atcha, Sahib*. We wait. We catch another Johnny!"

"Wait my foot! Come on! We'll drag him in and report. There will be a hell of a row! Better say it was an accident, or he died before we could get him in. . . ."

The Gurkha grinned.

"*Atcha, Sahib!*"

CHAPTER 11

Surrender!

There were indications all around us that the end was near. Attempts were now made by our air force to feed us from the air. The scheme was a hopeless failure. Aviation in those days, it should be remembered, was very much in its infancy, very much at the mercy of the weather. Certainly the tiny force in Iraq at the time of the siege was painfully inefficient. There were pilots who had by daring individual exploits in the work of aerial reconnaissance proved themselves invaluable, covered themselves with glory.

But to pay continuous visits to a beleaguered town and drop the necessary tons of foodstuffs on a given mark was another kettle of fish altogether. A 'plane would arrive, drop a sack or two into the town—grain, dates, packets of chocolates—and fly away. Then nothing happened for a day or two on account of high winds and rain squalls. Sometimes we had the agony of watching bags of sadly-needed food fall into the river. This manna from the skies would not have fed a decent-sized family for more than a fortnight, let alone the still considerable mob of us in the town of Kut. It was heart-breaking to see sacks of good food being carried down the swirling brown river. . . .

"The show's finished, Tiger. It's a question of hours now, I guess—certainly not more than a few days. We gotta prepare for it, old fellah. Get me?"

"Yes," I said wearily, "but how? Latifah's failed us. I tried again last night. Nobody around the Sink knows a thing about her."

"Aw, forget her! We've just gotta plan our way out."

"There isn't any way out—except as prisoners. And you know what that means! My God! I'll kill myself before I'll let those blasted swine use me for a—"

"Lay off that, Tiger, for the love of Pete! This is where we have to

118

keep a level head. I'm telling you! There must be a way out! Since that day when we talked about getting hold of Latifah so she could show us how she did it, I've thought of nothing else. I've come to the conclusion that she was lying, talking romantic, if you like. She's just the sort of kid that would. ..."

"Then how is it that she was able to get out and come back—and get away again?"

"We don't know that she did. All we know is that we'd been here some weeks before you spotted her in the bazaar, and that after seeing her a few times she disappeared again. In my opinion, she was never out of the place. She was just under cover, I guess."

"Then she's still here?"

"Sure! Still here—dead or alive! Maybe dead. But it was her association with the dive that gave me the idea. It sorta grew on me. Remember that Assyrian dame I was hot on? Satani, or whatever her moniker is—she's still down there. Christian same as us. The kid knows we're through. They all know. When Johnny walks in, she's going to dive for cover. Got me? Then, when the chance comes, she'll get out—push off across the desert to Persia, maybe."

"And we go with her?"

"Don't be a sap!" complained Steve. "We couldn't hide behind the wench's skirt, could we? But we can use the same hideout as she does—until our chance comes. The trouble is, we shan't be alone. Why, I guess half the boys are planning right now how they can escape Johnny. D'ya think they want to fall into his hands any more'n you do? Look at 'em! Every other fellah has become as crafty as Old Nick himself! One way or another, there's going to be a devil of a crowd missing when Johnny lines up his prisoners for the big trek. An' d'ya blame 'em?"

"It's every man for himself now. I can see that."

"Sure. The ship's sinking and we're all rattin'. A lot of 'em will be rounded up in the desert sooner or later, because Johnny's spread himself all over the damned place. And, by God! The last state will be worse than the first."

"Well, for heaven's sake!"

"Mighty soon the Union Jack is coming down and the white sheet is going up. As soon as that happens, we beat it for the dive. I picked up a couple of German Mausers in the *bazaar* soon after we got in, and a few rounds—and I still have 'em. How's that for preparations?"

"They'll be useful, of course."

"And what's more—don't shave from now on, kid. As a prisoner with the Turks that fairy dial of yours would damn you from the word 'go!'"

"It sounds a bit wild to me. I don't see how we can pull it off."

"Please yourself, Tiger. If you want to be a skirt for Johnny. . . ."

"You make me sick!"

"You'll be more than sick if you don't take a sporting chance. We may be caught. On the other hand, we may make a getaway. Anyway, it's worth trying. It's going to be hell trekking the desert with an army of Turks. I've trekked deserts. *I know!* Most of the fellahs are half-dead now! Have you thought of distances? Not on your sweet life, you ain't! The trek to Baghdad will be bad enough. But we shan't stay there. Johnny's in Mosul, and that's where we'll march to. An' if there's any of us left on our feet by that time, we'll hoof it across deserts and mountains to Constantinople. An' it's more than a thousand miles from Mosul to the Turkish capital. You see, Tiger, *I* didn't leave school to join this outfit. I've trekked around for a number of years, an' I guess I know my way about."

"Isn't the prospect bad enough without all this?"

"Don't you want to face facts?"

"What about Joe?"

"I doubt whether the little cockney will come out of dock before Johnny gets in. He's in better case than us. He'll be one of the precarious sick that'll be exchanged for Turkish prisoners of war over this surrender stunt. He ain't been any good since the trek from Ctesiphon."

"Poor devil!"

"There's a lot of 'em, Tiger. You can't play mother and father to an army."

We had to leave it at that for the nonce. But I never thought so hard in my life as I did in those ensuing days. There was no question about it—the show was all over. One could see the stark fact in the faces of the men as they went about their various tasks. Tommy has a reputation for always joking and singing in times of adversity. He had done a devil of a lot of joking and singing in those five horrible months in Kut. But there are limits in everything. He wasn't joking any more.

I think we put "paid" to it all after the incident of the *Julnar*. This was a gunboat that tried to run the blockade. She tried to come up the river to Kut. Those naval boys must have known they could get through only by a miracle, that all the odds were in favour of being shot to pieces. But they tried. They tried to bring us a boatload of food, comforts and medical supplies. They tried because of our report that men were dying at the rate of twenty a day from dysentery, scurvy, fevers and starvation.

On the night of April 24-25 we heard the roar of big guns and the rattle of musketry. It seemed to go on for hours. It came nearer—travelling along the river towards us—and we knew that a little gunboat with her gallant and heroic crew was trying to blaze her way through a terrific enfilade of bursting shells and withering fire. Then the awful silence that told its own tale. At dawn we saw the gunboat lying on her side by the river bank.

We knew that if we did not get out soon—we should all lie down and die.

Most of the boys were just standing skeletons held together by military equipment—or was it military discipline? From April 15 onwards we existed on a diet of four ounces of flour and a slice of horse or mule per man per day.

Before the end the daily death-rate averaged eight British and twenty-one Indians. These figures can be verified by reference to the Official History of the Mesopotamian Campaign.

I know that it was painful in the extreme to see some of the Indians. They would walk slowly to their lines, like men terribly, terribly tired, lie down, and die. Their pale brown faces were turned a dirty grey. They died from sheer exhaustion.

Every one of our horses was used—artillery, transport, cavalry, officers' chargers. Every mule and every donkey was slaughtered. Mule as a food, by the way, isn't so bad as it sounds. It produces more and sweeter fat than the horse. There was one particular mule that had been on three Indian Frontier Campaigns and wore the ribbons round its neck. The butchers refused to slaughter it. The animal was sent back to the stables four times. But in the end it had to go. The stench from the kitchens at this time was positively frightful. If we had not been so hungry the stench would have been enough to feed us!

I think that of all the units in Kut the tough little Gurkhas stood the strain best. They had no scruples about horseflesh like their Indian brothers. They ate it from the beginning and enjoyed it. Those fellows would enjoy anything. For sheer endurance there are no soldiers in the world to beat them. Everyone knows of their wonderful righting records on the various fronts during the Great War. Freezing in Flanders or sweltering in Arabia or Africa—it was all the same to them. They have a reserve of stamina that is nothing short of astounding. In Kut they fought and laboured uncomplainingly to the end. It seems worth repeating that the Gurkha is the only native soldier permitted in canteens used by British troops; but this fact has far more significance in caste-ridden India than in any other part of the world.

After the failure of the 'planes to supply us with rations, they began to come over with cigarettes and tobacco, but even these luxuries could not be delivered in sufficient quantities to supply all the troops. General Townshend would have no privileges. He stopped the supplies by wireless. The Tommies themselves tried all manner of things in their efforts to satisfy the craving for a smoke, which, in such desperate circumstances, is infinitely greater than under normal conditions. Some of the results were poisonous! An unmentionable mixture was wrapped in leaves. One could smell this home-made brand several yards away!

As the end drew near another batch of fellows tried the river. Many who could swim braved the swirling torrents under cover of night. A number of Arabs went the same way. I've seen them drop silently into the water, using skin bladders, and in a few seconds the current had swept them away.

During that last week men were constantly disappearing. Most of them were shot at and drowned. Some few, however, managed to get through to the relief force downstream. They reached their destination only after being peppered with shrapnel and bullets, and many of them were maimed for life. Even so, they must have prided themselves on that feat of superhuman endurance, especially when they later heard the tale of atrocities and bestialities and mutilations that made up the lot of the besieged garrison when it was taken over by the enemy.

There were 2,680 British troops taken at Kut. By the time the Armistice was signed with Turkey 1,306 of these had perished and 449 remained untraced. Of the 10,486 Indians, combatants and followers, 1,290 perished also without fighting, and 1,773 were never traced. They left a trail of whitening bones along that awful road from Kut to Baghdad, from the city of the Caliphs to Mosul, from that god-forsaken town in Upper Mesopotamia to Afion Kara Hissar in Asia Minor, even on to Aleppo and Constantinople itself.

In the whole history of the British Army there never was a surrender on the same scale as the Surrender of Kut. There were nearly nine thousand combatants, without reckoning the followers, surrendered at Kut. The only historical instance that in any way approaches this was the surrender of Cornwallis with 7,070 troops in the American War of Independence.

General Townshend issued his last *communiqué* to the troops on April 28, the day before the actual surrender. Even then he had not given up hope of saving his men:

> These considerations alone, namely, that I can help my comrades of all ranks to the end, have decided me to overcome my bodily illness and the anguish of mind which I am suffering now, and I have interviewed the Turkish General-in-Chief yesterday, who is full of admiration at 'an heroic defence of five months,' as he puts it. Negotiations are still in progress, but I hope to be able to announce your departure for India, on parole not to serve against the Turks, since the Turkish commander says he thinks it will be allowed, and has wired to Constantinople to ask for this, and that the *Julnar*, which is lying with food for us at Magasis, may be permitted to come to us. Whatever has happened, my comrades, you can only be proud of yourselves. We have done our duty to King and Empire; the whole world knows that we have done our duty. I ask you to stand by me with your steady and splendid discipline, shown throughout, in the next few days for the expedition of all service I demand of you.

Townshend ought to have known the Turks better. I doubt if any man among us believed in the possibility of a parole. There was of course no question of such a release. We were taken into captivity, and no army of men has ever suffered greater humiliation, more fiendish brutality, nor yet more atrocious and sadistic behaviour at the hands of their captors than the gallant men of Kut.

An offer of £1,000,000 later increased to £2,000,000, together with our forty-one guns, failed to tempt the Turks in this matter of release on parole. We were to give them, too, an equal number of fit and healthy Turkish prisoners of war in exchange for our sick and wounded. "These would be honourable terms," says the Official History of the Mesopotamian Campaign, "such as the Austrians had allowed Massena at the siege of Genoa in 1800, and were also the same as had been allowed by the British to the French in 1808 in Portugal."

It was not to be. On April 29, 1916, the Union Jack came down and the white flag went up. We were ready to surrender. We had no food left. We destroyed all our guns, most of the ammunition, the stores of equipment, harness and the like, threw the bolts of our rifles in the river, made a bonfire of everything that could be burned, and sank what few boats we had left at the river bank outside the town.

Shortly after noon on that memorable day a Turkish regiment marched on the fort to take over the guards in Kut. At one pip emma our radio signalled "Goodbye!" to those who had tried to help us, who had fought for so long to relieve us, and then the wireless was destroyed.

We had 1,450 sick and wounded in hospital, 1,136 of these, the more precarious cases, were at once exchanged for healthy Turkish prisoners of war.

On that day the Kut garrison started to march up the river to Shumran camp, about eight miles. The troops were moving out for three days, and though many were unfit to march eight yards let alone eight miles, no food was issued to the starving troops until the second day. Then each man was given a biscuit. This article was about four inches in circumference and three-quarters of an inch thick. Iron rations with a vengeance! These biscuits were so hard that it took several hours of soaking in water to render them fit for chewing by the strongest teeth! This is not a cheap joke. It is a statement of fact.

It took the better part of four days to assemble the Kut prisoners at Shumran camp—and during that time three hundred men died!

The rank and file were separated from the officers. General Townshend left Kut by steamer for Baghdad *en route* for Constantinople on May 3, and reached his destination a month later.

On May 4 the first batch of British and Indian officers were sent up the river to Baghdad by steamer. They were followed a few hours later by the remainder of the officers. It is true that the officers protested vigorously against this preferential treatment. The Turks merely shrugged their shoulders. They could not understand officers bothering about the rank and file.

Nevertheless, had the officers insisted on remaining with their men and marching with them to Baghdad, that trek would not have been the appallingly brutal one that in fact it was. With their officers alongside them the rank and file would not have suffered bestial treatment from Turk and Arab irregular, and there would have been fewer dying men left by the wayside to rot in the sun.

The men of Kut, weak and exhausted and starved by the long siege had to march one hundred miles to Baghdad. The hot season was just beginning. There were no tents for prisoners. Many were without kits or blankets. By the time the trek began many were without shoes to their feet, having traded them for a handful of dates, a bit of black bread and a pair of Arab sandals. They did not want the sandals, but they did want the bread. Both Turkish and Arab troops went around peddling their own rations in order to get possession of a good pair of British boots or a greatcoat.

That ill-fated column started its terrible trek on May 6, 1916.

CHAPTER 12

The Trek to Baghdad

We found it easy enough to get under cover. Naturally there was a great deal of confusion when the Turks marched into Kut. Our great difficulty was to get from under cover again! The Turkish troops swarmed all over the place. In a few hours the town was a ghastly sight—far more tragic than we had ever known it. We emerged one dark night to scout around and see how the land lay. We found the streets littered with dead Arabs, men and women. They had been stripped of their clothing. Scores of them were hanging by the neck from timbers that jutted out of the *façades* of the buildings. They hung from the doors of shops and from the roof beams of the *bazaar*, some of them head downwards.

Johnny jabbed at the swinging bodies with his bayonet as he passed by. The bodies were terribly emaciated and incredibly skinny, especially the women; and they must not have required much hanging for life to pass out. Johnny was rude with his stabbing, displaying a frightfully bestial mind.

"*Canaille!*" spat a Turkish officer, chopping about with his sabre to his little heart's content.

We did, as a matter of fact, very nearly run into him! In spite of the dead blackness of the night, we had one or two very close shaves, for the Turkish troops wandered about all night long, working their will on male and female alike and then murdering them.

There were no children among the victims. Johnny had spared them—for his own use. It is disastrous to be a female and young when the Turk is on the warpath. It made no difference that these were fellow Moslems. The truth of the matter is that the Turk never really embraced the faith of Islam. He merely pretended to for political reasons. The Turk has no faith.

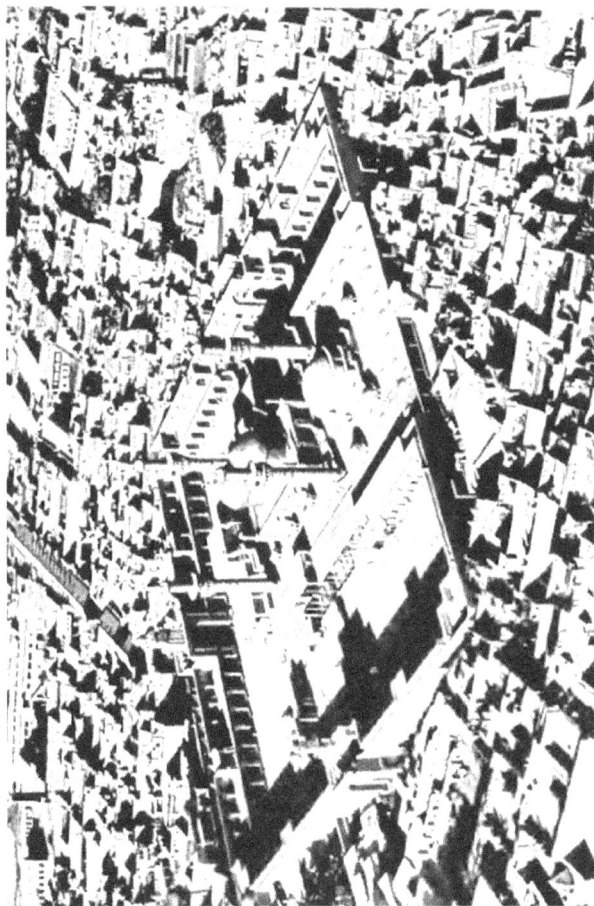

The Baghdad of our dreams
A remarkable aerial view of the Kazamaine Mosque

We came upon women crumpled up in the gutter, old and those not yet old—and one in particular that I shall never forget. That episode convinced me beyond all possibility of argument that the Turk is the world's most cruel and most atrocious sadist.

We had pulled up suddenly in the shadow of a courtyard. Not many yards from us was a group of vociferous Turks around a screaming woman.

There were women, no longer possessed of the bloom of youth, with terrible wounds and even worse mutilations; men butchered in ways unmentionable. I write of what I saw. These are things that never fade from the memory, however eventful one's later life may be.

And the crime of these town Arabs of Kut? Friendliness towards the British! Ye gods! When their only crime was that they had elected to stay in the town and starve with us! All their *kow-towing* obeisances before the conquering Turk had apparently availed them nothing. Johnny had been turned loose about the dirty highways and byways to vent his spleen on all and sundry. The result was wholesale rape and slaughter.

We caught three of them in a dark alley. They seemed to have got adrift from their companions. Two held down an Arab boy while the third committed the unspeakable crime. We used our Mausers—since we had the Turks where we wanted them. Then we took to our heels, for the shots echoed and re-echoed through the streets. These troops were fresh in the country, and we knew the cellarage of Kut! There was some satisfaction in having got three of the victorious Turks.

(Today one can read in the Official History of this phase of the campaign in Mesopotamia that representations were made on behalf of the starving Arabs at the time of the surrender by British officials. The officials received the curt reply that the Arabs were Turkish subjects and would be dealt with accordingly. Johnny appears to have had the insolence to state that he could not spare any food!)

It is an insult to swine to give the Turk such a name. The whole world knows about his wholesale massacre of the Armenians in 1895-6, when a three-days killing began with the sound of a horn and ended after several hundreds of men, women and children had been shot, stabbed and bludgeoned to death. But what does the world know of the bludgeonings and bayonetings of the half-starved British lads who staggered along the roads to Baghdad, to Mosul, to Ras-el-Ain in Asia Minor, to Aleppo, through months of blinding heat during the hot season of 1916?

Not twenty *per cent* of the twelve thousand or so British and Indian soldiers taken captive at Kut lived to tell the tale when the war was all over. And of the survivors—some are still in Asia Minor! Up to a few years ago, (as at time of first publication), they were still making their way home to India. Among the bandits that infest the mystery hills and valleys of Northern Arabia in these days there are men of British and Indian blood. Later in the Great War, after the advance on Baghdad and Mosul, thousands of Turks also took to the hills. It has been estimated that at one time there were no fewer than 300,000 Turks alone roaming Asia Minor, preying on town and village, robbing, pillaging, slaughtering. . . .

It may be a long time since the close of the Great War, but the effects of it still remain, for outlawry and banditry is as much alive today as in the days when the *Caliphs* reigned. The historic highways across the top of Arabia are still the hunting-grounds of the wildest cutthroats and marauders—Kurds, Arabs, Turks, Indians and Britishers. A tragic legacy of the Great War in the Near East. Hence the presence in those regions of the equally daring bands of desert police—the Iraq Desert Patrols.[1]

Trekking north to the hills was one way of escape from the brutalities of the Turks, and not a few attempted it in those awful days of 1916. Steve Barry and I might well have been among the number. We had prepared an escape. We had no idea of what lay beyond Kut. There was Baghdad and Mosul in the north, the Persian border to the east; but it was all very vague. For us it was a blind escape just as for hundreds of others. We might have ended up in the hills and become bandits from self-preservation—since in those mystery regions raiding is the only industry man knows.

We did not make good our escape. The reason was woman. In the hideout were two of the species—Satani and Latifah. Steve was right. (Amazing how often that fellow was right!) Latifah was still in the town and very much alive. If there were any way out of the benighted place she was never able to locate it. There ought to have been a better scope for her romantic temperament than such a spot afforded. But fate doesn't ask us where we'd like to be born nor where she shall pitch us. And it was no good rating that lovely and mysterious creature for a little liar. I fancy she just couldn't help behaving as she did.

There might have been a chance for us if we had not bothered about these dames, as Steve phrased it. But the night came when we

---

1. See *Hell Riders* by same Author.

129

had to get out for Johnny was getting in! We made for the brick kilns that night. It was pitch black and there seemed to be an impression that we could get along the river bank from that point, and then away across the desert to the Persian border and, for these two women, the safety of the Sabian family of whom Latifah had spoken. After which Steve and I would make our way down to Basrah. That was the plan. But—*the best laid schemes of mice and men. . . .*

Perhaps, if the dames had not bothered about us they would not have met such a sticky end. Who knows? Who shall say in such a world of uncertainties?

We reached the river bank—the four of us. The water was subsiding. But it was still too much of a proposition for us indifferent swimmers. We had to move along the bank to the north-east until we came to the bend in the river, then straight into the desert. So much we knew. The rest must be a more or less blind dash into the mysterious blackness.

We must have been going along the edge of the stream for the better part of an hour when we pulled up suddenly. A figure loomed up out of the darkness—or at all events, the light of his cigarette gave him away. There was a distant sound of voices. We could not hope to get away without running the gauntlet somewhere. It looked as if we must pass a Turkish post or camp.

Crouching in the mud of that bank with a couple of women was not exactly thrilling. I'd rather have crouched there without them. So, too, would Steve. It was done now. There could be no turning back. There was only one way—forward! But first we must remove this fellow with the cigarette. We dared not use the Mausers. A jack-knife would serve. These girls had knives too—so we discovered! There ensued an argument, none the less fierce because it was carried on in whispers, as to who should strike the blow. In the end Steve suddenly leapt forward. We saw the light of that cigarette swirl round, heard a stifled cry, a scuffle and a thud as the two men went down. Then silence. We lay there hardly daring to breathe, wondering how far that muffled cry had carried.

Steve came up on hands and knees. I remember his pause, the mere detail of his pushing the knife in the dirt to clean the blade.

"Come on!" he said.

We went on, crouching low, stepping carefully over the body, and we knew by the sound of things that we were drawing nearer to a Turkish post. The night was all in our favour, but how near the stream were these guards? The query was soon answered. There were two of them squatting by the water's edge, staring at the river, rifles across their knees. We sat down too—and perspired. We knew that if we were caught now these Johnnies would have little mercy on us and less on the women.

But, as Steve said, we had to go some place before daylight! To turn away from the river at this point was even more fatal. (How did the Arabs manage to get past our double-armed sentries and steal rifles from under us while we slept? Such things occurred repeatedly in British camps all over Mesopotamia. Tickle a man to make him turn in his sleep?)

At that stage we were not very adept at the cat-like tread. After all, we had been in the country but a short eighteen months. Though it seemed like eighteen years since one had left one's home and school and had told lies at a recruiting office about one's age in a flush of patriotic excitement. So much for patriotism! It began to look as if we should have to slaughter our way out.

And then these child-women took a very decided part. It was a simple one. It was as old as the hills. It always works with certain types of men! Nothing will affect me very strongly any more. I sometimes think I had all my vital experiences during my crazy adolescence. It was amazing to me then, not to say nauseating, to remain crouched there and watch those girls get to work on those two dim figures of men. True, the men responded with like rapidity. It was all so cold-blooded and quiet and disgustingly business-like! Our part was to pounce upon the two Johnnies while thus engaged. . . .

Nothing could have been easier to us two desperate men. After all, it was our lives or theirs. You cannot bring the moral reasonings of civilisation to such instances as these. They are beyond ordinary human conception. They call for swift and decisive action. We pounced upon them where they lay. No two men could have been more totally unaware than they. Someone once wrote that man's sole aim in life is the seeking of happiness and the avoidance of pain. Certainly those two sought happiness according to their own crooked lights. The pain was swift and sure.

Satani and Latifah helped us to roll them softly down the bank and into the water. Their rifles went with them. We had no use for such dangerous weapons. We had enough to do to secret the Mausers about our persons.

I suppose we must have presented a weird sight. We were caked in mud. But we had taken the precaution to clothe ourselves well before we started out. The original scheme had been to garb ourselves with *haik* and *burnous* after the manner of the Arab, but when we saw what was happening to the Arabs of Kut during our nights' excursions into the streets, we quickly changed our ideas. One had a better chance as a Tommy than as a native! Though it would have been difficult to tell what we were by the time we had set forth.

We had emerged from that dive looking like a couple of canteen *wallahs*—non-combatants who wore a sort of semi-officer's uniform. It was the girls who had procured the skirted tunics with "patch" pockets, the breeches and puttees. I suspected they had been removed from dead officers by marauding Arabs at some time or other. They were, of course, devoid of badges, epaulettes or any other insignia of rank. This outfit, by the way, was to serve us in good stead later on.

As for my personal appearance—"With that wisp of ginger moustache and imperial, Tiger, you look like a tame artist from Greenwich Village dressed up as a canteen *wallah!*"

By the time we had belly-crawled a mile or two along the mud of the river bank the description could have been improved. After depositing the two sentries we started forward again. We came into full view of the Turkish post. There were five or six men there and immediately beyond a whole camp of troops. The post was some twenty yards from the bank. It was possible to get by. We had to risk what might lie further ahead.

Steve led the way as we crawled along, pursuing a path as near the edge of the stream as we could. All went well until Satani slipped in the mud and sat down at the water's edge with a resounding splash! I bit off a few hot words. And that made matters worse. We crouched half-in and half-out of the water and listened to the sounds of running feet. I realised with a sinking dread that the feet were coming towards us.

"What the hell are we sitting here for!" snarled Steve. "Come on! Keep away from the water."

We started to run, Steve in front, the two women next, while I tailed in the rear. A figure loomed up in front of our leader. His fist shot out and the figure toppled over and slid down the bank.

"Don't shoot!" snapped Steve, as we raced along.

Other figures loomed up out of the darkness. I saw Satani lunge with knife in hand. Johnny dropped to his knees. Again! And another went down. Latifah too! I struck at the nearest with the Mauser-butt.

The night was suddenly filled with cries. It was imperative that we should silence this handful of men before the rest of the camp was roused.

We all knew what it must mean if we were caught now! Two *Nasrani*. Two prisoners—also Christians! That's the sort of knowledge that makes a fellow fight until he drops. Better that we should finish now than be caught. . . . to fall into the hands of these enraged Turks! There could not be anything worse than that.

Guards came up at the double. We clubbed with the rifles snatched from the men at our feet. God! How those two women fought! It was deadly. It was silent. Two wild cats fighting tooth and claw, gasping and snorting as if they had run many miles. But never a word to express the blazing hate in their eyes. Lunging with those dripping knives. No Johnny attempted to shoot. That, we knew, would be too easy a death for us! In that, too, lay our slender chance. . . . If we could break through these guards who seemed intent on taking us alive, jabbing with their bayonets.

Terror walked my brain then. They should not take me alive if I had to fight the whole camp. Terror lent deadly aim to the whirling rifle. Then Latifah went down . . . went down with a choking sob . . . skull cracked. I went completely off the rails. My eyes filled with blood as if they would burst.

I have no clear recollection of what happened after the girl had dropped, a dead thing, at my feet. I know only that she had leapt with her knife and taken the blow that was aimed at me. How could I remember anything after that? I knew then the meaning of blood-lust. I wanted passionately to have the blood of these devils running in pools at my feet. Nothing short of that would avenge this ghastly thing they had done.

This child-woman. I had known the warm folds of her bosom. I had seen blood gush from her soft mouth. She was cold. I saw red—blood-red. I knew an insane desire for murder. Hot-blooded passion swept me then as I hope it never will again. I went on beating at the last of the guards where he lay—until Steve dragged me off.

"Come on, you little runt! We gotta run for it!"

"Latifah!"

"She's finished. We can't do anything. Come on, for God's sake!"

I picked the girl up in my arms. She was heavy in death. The once-lovely face was nothing but a patch of blood. Steve dragged me to my feet. We broke into a run with Satani between us. I don't know how long we kept it up. It may have been an hour or three hours. I knew that we had cleared the camp, left it well behind . . . left what was left of Latifah behind. We were running blindly into the desert and there didn't seem to be anything to stop us. Once I pitched headlong into a hole. When I staggered to my feet the other two were yards ahead. I ran on and on, sobbing like a kid. In that reaction I hadn't any guts left. I wanted to lie down and die.

"Tiger! For God's sake, pull yourself together!"

All this time Satani had not uttered a word. Cockney Joe was right. She could not have been more aptly named. There was something terribly savage about Satani. She may have been an Assyrian Christian, but she had the instincts of a Bedouin woman. She'd never cry over spilt blood. Perhaps her mode of life. . . . Maybe she had fought her way out of hell before.

Then she tumbled headlong into the dirt and stayed there. We started to shake her, thinking she was just played out and demanding a rest.

"*Imshi!*" she said, in a throaty sort of gurgle, using the Arabic imperative for "go!"

It was all she ever did say. Steve's hand came away from her neck smeared in blood. He spat an ejaculation then of such frightful potency that it cannot be repeated. Two words to reveal a man's state as no other words could. Love didn't enter into it—not with a hard-bitten *wallah* like Steve. But he must have come as near to that strange state as a man of his calibre ever could. I think I was more astounded with this revelation than at the death of the girl.

"How'n hell did she run . . . in this state?"

How—save that her one remaining instinct had urged her on. Horror of what would happen to her if she fell wounded into the hands of the unspeakable Turk. That had kept her going. That had kept her on her feet while she ran, making a trail of her blood. When life had drained from her she could run no more.

"Satani," said Steve, as if, in this emotional state so alien to his make-up, he did not know the words.

We carried her back to the hole into which I had stumbled a few yards away, laid her down in it, and pushed the dirt over her with our hands.

We wandered away, further and further into the darkness. It seemed that it would never be daylight any more. We knew no direction, did not want to know any. It was enough that we trudged on, kept going. What was there to do? Where was there to go, anyway? We had started out with two women—two souls who had brought comfort and something resembling happiness at times when life was drear and hopeless and a lingering death by starvation was the only thing that the future seemed to hold. You can't forget such women in a hurry— even women like Satani and Latifah whom the world pretends to despise. They were lovely women who could do lovely things to a man when life was damnable. And if the world despises the class, so much the worse for the world.

There wasn't anything more to the night, except an aimless, shiftless, futile wandering. There wasn't anything else to do. There wasn't anything to say. We trudged on. Two of God's most wretched creatures. And when we could not stagger any further we lay down in the dirt and slept like logs.

No two men ever had a more rude awakening. I know I awoke to grab instinctively at something that was jabbing into my buttocks. It was cold steel. It was a bayonet. The other end of it was in the hands of a powerful-looking Turk bending over me. I leapt to my feet. We started cussing each other. A jab from the fellow's rifle-butt sent me staggering and brought full realisation of where I was. I stared round. Steve was telling two more Johnnies what he thought about them. They did not understand, even though his language was both sanguinary and descriptive.

The horrible truth slowly penetrated our dull wits. *We had caught up with the column of British prisoners trekking to Baghdad!* Our night's wandering had been a detour of many miles. We must have drifted around for fifteen or twenty miles. The long straggling column was drifting by. We stared at them, unable to believe our own eyesight. The Kut garrison, we later learned, had started early that morning from Shumran. Actually we had been ahead of the column!

"I suppose it had to be," I said miserably.

"Of all the saps! We would hang around with a couple of dames!"

The morning after the tragic night before! May 6, 1916.

On they came, hundreds of them in a column miles and miles long, British lads taken prisoners, with Turkish and Arab soldiery heavily armed marching alongside, mounted Turkish and German officers riding up and down the ragged ranks. We made no attempt to join them, continued to argue with our bewildered captors—until an officer rode up and asked what we had fallen out for and why hadn't we been driven back into the column.

Then, like Johnny, he noticed our mud-spattered uniforms, mistook us for officers, asked why we had not gone up the river in the steamers, and for what reason we had removed our badges of rank! He spoke French with a German accent. Steve took over the *pow-wow* and spoke French and Arabic at him with American idioms thrown in. It was marvellous the amount of satisfaction that Steve could get off his tongue. When he reached that point where it was impossible for him to express his feelings in an alien tongue, he used plain, unvarnished American. We had fallen out for an obvious reason, didn't the blankety-blank-blank German-cum-Turkey officer's kidneys ever let him down? If we chose to march to Baghdad with these brave fellahs—what in hades had that to do with any ten-cent officer who happened along on a horse, with dreadful emphasis on the horse?

Steve's language was a trifle mixed. In other circumstances it might have been quite humorous. The officer suspected he was being guyed. His face flushed a deep purple. His eyes blazed. He slashed out with his crop, yelling the while to the guards to drive us into the column and keep us there. The guards, Turks and Arabs, drove us into line with their bludgeons and rifle-butts.

Thus we began the march to Baghdad. We fell in at the rear of the column—which is the worst possible place to be in, for the sun came up and roasted the face of the desert until it was a foot deep in grey dust. This was kicked up by thousands of feet and a great many hoofs into a huge cloud—a cloud through which we marched all day long.

"Don't worry, Tiger. Baghdad's only a hundred miles away. I guess we can think up something before we get there!"

It looked like an impossible situation to me. We should never be able to break away from this mob. There were far more Turks and Arabs than Britishers. That was necessary, I suppose, otherwise we should have made a little war on our own before that first day of marching had passed. Worn and exhausted as the men were, they were jibed and goaded beyond endurance. If a man fell out he was lashed unmercifully, jabbed with bayonets, kicked back into the column.

But it was not too bad that first day. There were occasional halts when we were allowed to lie down in our tracks. We were issued with iron rations that had been sent up stream by our own people, the force that had tried to relieve us. Our captors had agreed that we should not be marched for more than eight hours a day. Though how on earth the British authorities could agree to eight hours a day for men in such an exhausted condition is beyond me.

That condition obtained for only one day, however, for as soon as Johnny got us out and away from any possible observation by our air force, he marched us, not till we dropped, but from daylight to dark every day for eight days. If those who dropped out could not be driven into the ranks again with bludgeons, whips and bayonets, they were left in the desert to rot or to fall into the hands of the brown women who tailed us like vultures.

When you're wounded and left on Arabia's (?) plains,
And the women come out to cut up what remains.
Just roll to your rifle and blow out your brains,
An' go to your Gawd like a soldier.

Only our Tommies didn't have any rifles. The condition of the men, the forced marching, the iron rations and the brutal treatment brought on the inevitable dysentery. Only those who have suffered dysentery on the march, or seen others suffering can appreciate the hell of it. A man might continue to stagger along while he relieved himself in other ways. Men did often enough. But dysentery is different. Such cases had to drop out, suffer the most excruciating pain, then struggle to join the ranks again.

The Arab and the Turk have a warped sense of humour. It became a game with them to spot the dysentery cases. We passed men who had dropped out of the column ahead of us. They lay crouching on their sides, rear exposed and bleeding not so much from dysentery as from bayonet stabs. During that appalling eight-days' nightmare we left hundreds of men lying in the desert, dysentery cases that had fallen out in the hope that they would catch up again within a few minutes, but because of the atrocious treatment by each passing Turk and Arab guard they were never able to rise again. The women who came up from the desert villages did the rest.

In the beginning Steve and I had tried to help these fellows back to the ranks. We succeeded in dragging a few back to the column, in spite of the lashing of the guards. Other men fell out to help their comrades, but the disorder became such that the guards drove us back with fixed bayonets. Sometimes we dragged a man along for miles, his clothing sodden with the blood of that dreadful disease, screaming with the pain of his desire—until we had to let him go—to take his chance outside the column.

A man would suddenly become light-headed with the strain, with the incessant marching, the ferocious brutality, the incredible things done before his eyes. We would take his arms and help him along. Then the dragging stage. This would bring a guard up with his rhino-hide crop. The man who was by his sickness delaying the column would be torn from us, and as we passed on we could hear his piteous cries as the guards beat him into insensibility.

When we reached Azizieh, the majority of us more dead than alive, it was dusk and we lay down in our tracks. The whole body refused to move another inch. We were given black bread and a few dates and allowed to fill our water bottles. Azizieh lies about half-way between Kut and Baghdad. When morning came we still refused to move. The guards used their whips and sticks freely enough. But still we refused to rise. I know that I was as stiff as a board, with a head like lead, in-credibly dirty—for we were given no opportunity to clean ourselves. But my state was nothing. I did not have dysentery, and, miraculously the malaria did not return. The intolerable pains in the head were due to the strains of the past four days and exposure to the heat. I was dreading heat stroke.

Even so, my state was nothing. Steve and I were fortunate in that we started out with good boots on our feet, well clothed, and un-troubled with any of these dread diseases. Those poor devils who had traded their boots for bread were now suffering the tortures of the damned. The Arab sandals they wore were in shreds. Some had torn up their shirts in order to bind aching and blistered feet.

It was a strange mutiny that we put up. There had been no organi-sation about it, no agreement among ourselves. We just hid our heads and cursed when the guards came with their whips—and remained lying on the ground. At last a number of officers came up. They told us that we must march on to Baghdad, that there was no food for us in Azizieh. We told them in uncertain French and bastard Arabic that we needed a day's rest, that proper provision must be made for the sick. We refused point-blank to move until the sick had been attended to, until we had had an opportunity to clean ourselves, and until we had rested one day at least.

The result was that we remained at Azizieh for the day, the sick were carted away to some dilapidated and insanitary buildings; but at least they were allowed to rest away from the blazing heat. They had a chance to attend to themselves. We left 250 of them behind at Azizieh when we resumed the march next morning.

Crowds of Arabs rolled up during the day from the outlying vil-lages. They came round us where we sat, staring or rather leering at us, spitting in our faces, making lunatic gestures as they drew fingers across their throats, implying an even more rude demise with their knives . . . especially the women. They had not had such an opportunity for sadistic anticipations in years! White men, exasperated beyond endurance, leapt and struck at the grinning hags—only to be beaten to their knees by the guards.

The remarks of the prisoners at this juncture would have blenched the cheeks of the most hardened hooligan. The things they spat at those jeering brown women can only be put down to the abnormal conditions under which they suffered. They could, if one were to judge by their utterances, have taught those dirty Arabs a great deal about the practice of mutilation.

What happened to those 250 sick after we left, God alone knows. They were supposed to follow us when sufficient barges had been collected to convey them up stream to Baghdad. We never made contact with them again. All we know is that when we set off again the pace was increased. The officers were evidently determined to make up for that one day lost. For the better part of that first day out from Azizieh we were driven along at a sort of jog-trot. We halted on the outskirts of a village and lay down in the dust for the night.

Those of us who still possessed blankets were comfortable enough. It is no hardship for men who had campaigned in that country for eighteen months to sleep on the ground. We were too worn and weary to bother about the bed in the dirt. To be in possession of a blanket was to sleep luxuriously. The real trouble started next day when men began to show signs of breaking under the pace. From a stumbling jog-trot we gradually fell into a crawl, and no amount of bullwhip or bludgeon could increase the pace. The welcome darkness came after another day of unspeakable tortures. We had left a few more men to die by the roadside.

There was little rest for us that night, however. A Turkish officer was shot. Somebody had put a bullet in his ear. The sound of the shot woke us all somewhere around midnight. In the confusion that followed I was concerned only about one thing—hiding my gun. We all knew what would happen. Every man would be searched. When we found out who the officer was we sent up a prayer of thankfulness to the mysterious one who had fired the bullet into his brain.

Most of the officers were easy enough. They were not actually brutal—leaving that to the guards—but merely indifferent, apathetic. The cruelties and atrocities that went on all around them did not seem to register with their dull wits. They were drinking most of the way and they had their own women and boy followers. The one who had been shot, however, was in different case. He had been looking for trouble ever since we started. He sought his amusements among the wretched prisoners. He had a way of looking at a young fellow, as some men look at women, feet upwards. The situation of his death told its own tale.

"Bury that rod, Tiger!" snapped Steve, as soon as he heard the shot. "These Turkey guys can't make up their minds whether we're officers or not, and the chances are they'll be down on us right now as the only fellows likely to have a rod."

We buried the incriminating things where we lay, scrabbling in the dirt feverishly with our hands. There were shouts and yells from all quarters of the camp. The guards were flogging the men into line, our clothes were torn open, blankets strewn around, kits scattered, personal belongings thrown all over the place in a desperate effort to find the man with the gun. The search went on all night. The score or so of men who were unlucky enough to be near the dead officer were bludgeoned and beaten until they were insensible. But no man talked. It is doubtful if any knew, except the one who had fired the shot, for it would be simple in that covering darkness. A number of guards who had been doing duty in that part of the line were placed under arrest, roped together and thrust in with the rest of us prisoners.

Dawn came and we buried the officer. A further search was made in the light of day. Anything might have been buried in that time. With the passing to and fro of men and guards the whole area of dusty plain had been churned, so that it was impossible to pick on any place for digging operations—though the officers were convinced that the gun had been buried.

They had to give it up in the end. The last lap to Baghdad was begun. That murder in the night seemed to have sobered a lot of the Turkish guards. Maybe they were afraid for their own skins. Naturally, a guard did not wish to make himself conspicuous by his ferocious behaviour and thus mark himself as the next man for attention. As for the Arab irregulars—nothing appeared to make any difference to them now that they had this exceptional opportunity for beating the *infidel* Christians. They kept it up right to the gates of Baghdad.

CHAPTER 13

Flogged Across Asia

What could the citizens of Baghdad think of the limping, ragged, dirty, unkempt, straggling column of British prisoners of war when we entered the city that has known tragedy and change for hundreds of centuries? We approached the historic capital by way of a nameless road to a crumbling bund—an earth mound that runs outside the city's boundary practically the whole way round.

A forest of minarets and domes rose up beside the river, out of the dun-coloured dust of the plains, as it were; and not all the rottenness of war could restrain the thrilling sensations of that first glimpse! We passed through walled fruit gardens and on to groves of date palms through the leafy tops of which the peacock blue and old gold of the domes and minarets gleamed. And one pictured "the golden prime of good Haroun Al-Raschid," the picturesque tales of the *Arabian Nights*, and all the romance and mournful beauty of the ancient city where the *Caliphs* had reigned.

I soon learned, of course, that the only colour in the architectural features of Baghdad is in the mosaic tiling of the mosques. For the rest, it is dun-coloured, dust-laden, reeking with decay. Even so, he would be a dull dog who could not find romance there. It is in the environs of the palace and the citadel, in the crowded *bazaars*, on the crumbling balconies where the women forgathered, at the coffee houses where the bearded patriarchs squat on high benches and surveyed us meditatively, in the arched and vaulted thoroughfares, and especially in the eyes above veiled faces that stared at one through the lattices and portcullises of the harem windows.

Dust and decay everywhere. Yet colour and romance, too. Even in the seething, sullen concourse that jeered at us, for there were masses of unveiled women and girls who scorned the drab and rusty black of their Moslem sisters—Armenian, Assyrian and Chaldean women who gazed at us with embarrassing boldness, whose big eyes were frank and friendly. It was the Arabs, men and women and children, who spat and guffawed as we trudged by.

The Arabs of Mesopotamia are a breed apart. They always *kowtowed* to the victor, yelled vile things at the vanquished. This mongrel breed, descendant of a mixed ancestry of Kurds, Persians, Jews, Turks, Syrians and heaven knows what, must not be confused with the independent Arab of Arabia proper a vastly different breed. These same Baghdad Arabs rushed forward to cheer and acclaim the victorious British when they entered the city two years later!

But even they and their jeering insults could not affect one's thrilling interest in the ancient capital, and for us tired and weary campaigners there was something reassuring and comforting about the silent attitude of the Christian element. They, too, were suffering. Their possessions had been confiscated, their churches taken from them, their women molested. Jews, Chaldeans, Armenians and Assyrians had fared ill at the hands of the Turkish despoilers. This we were soon to learn.

It was a memorable day. We had come five hundred miles from the sea, from Fao Fort where we had made that wild and ferocious landing eighteen months ago. And now, after all, we were come to Baghdad not as conquerors but as miserable prisoners of war. For this we had fought and sweated and suffered through many weary months! We were the famous garrison of Kut, starved into surrender by the Turks. It was not surprising that the yelling and booing was spasmodic, confined to a particular section of the staring throng. There were others who appeared nearer to tears than jeers.

We were marched through the city, up one street, down another, round the quadrangles, and back into the streets. Clearly we were on exhibition! The Turks were trying to impress the populace. The idea was to show the crowd just what abject wretches these British soldiers really were. It ought to have succeeded, for we certainly presented the appearance of being beaten. We were beaten to the world. There never was a column of more miserable-looking wretches than those ill-fated men of Kut. What would you? We had reached the limit of physical endurance. We who had killed 'em with shovels just limped into Baghdad.

At long last we were allowed to rest. Some of us found ourselves quartered in an Armenian church—or what had once been a church.

A STREET IN BAGHDAD SHOWING THE MAIDAN MOSQUE

It was difficult to tell what it was now. We were crowded into it like a lot of cattle. There were others already established there when we arrived—a huddle of persecuted Christians of both sexes and all ages. By the time the great doors were closed upon us the place was reminiscent of the Black Hole of Calcutta. The civilians were white people like ourselves—the white Christians of Asia.

We sat and stared at each other for a while in the gloom of that vaulted church. Here were women and girls and children with fair skins and the plaintive eyes of beaten dogs. This was Johnny's gesture towards the sex urge in men.

But Tommy is a good mixer. We were soon fraternising. In that cramped space, where men lay cheek by jowl with women whom they had never seen before, it would have been a feat of the greatest difficulty not to fraternise!

We gazed upon the girls, round, sentient, warm in friendliness, fair of face, fellows with a fellow feeling wondrous kind—and in such striking contrast to the black bundles of taunting brown women who had spat in our faces during the past eight unforgettable days. British soldiers, filthy beyond description, sat on the floor of that church with children on their knees and talked in their own affectionate, cussword fashion to the homeless mites.

"Hey, you little Blighter, what's your name? Sassoo! That' a funny one. Which is your mother—you know, mother, mama? That one? That one over there . . . smiling? You know, smiling? Like this." And Tommy would grin all over his jowl like a Cheshire cat.

"Blimey! The little bitch is just skin and bone! Johnny Turk no good, eh? Here! See what you can do with this." And Tommy parted with his last piece of dog biscuit.

The church was dim but not hushed. In fact it was soon a babble of chattering tongues. The children were immensely amused with Tommy's linguistic efforts. There was a little girl not more than eight or nine years sitting comfortably in Steve's lap. It was the funniest thing imaginable. The two were trying to carry on a conversation with signs and gestures. They would point to things and give them names, each in his or her own *patois*. The game soon became intensely interesting. Some of us gathered round Steve and his little friend whom he insisted on calling Satani!—and watched progress. It was certainly one way of learning the other fellow's language!

Their Arabic was more comprehensive than ours. They had learned it in a hard school. One realised from the choice of words that fell from the lips of these children that they had not acquired the language in quite the best circles. It was mostly gutter Arabic and pretty awful at that. The children blasphemed in Arabic without understanding, of course, the full meaning of the terms they used. I suspect that the English they acquired was not much better. The average soldier's language is a product apart, an argot born of an environment alien to most decent human instincts.

These children, thrown by fate into the maelstrom of war, knew more of life at the age of eight than our own sisters did at eighteen. Pathetic little old women! Already sexual stress and perversion were known to them. Their knowledge even shocked some of the Tommies.

"Hey, little Satani! Wouldn't I like to take you home to show the folks!"

In one Steve Barry it was the rarest bit of sentiment. His big, leathery jowl was creased in the happiest of smiles, just as if he had not a care in the world. The role of family man was new but not unfitting. In my astonishment I said as much.

"Gee! who could hurt a little kid like this, huh? Say! Satani! Where's your pop? Huh? Pop? Papa?"

The child drew a grubby finger across her throat and spat. The gesture became quite a familiar one in those regions.

"Gone home, huh? Too bad!"

"Gonnome?"

"Yeah. Finished. Dead!"

"*Oui*. Dead, dead, dead!"

The linguistic exercises were kept up until late evening, when the church doors were suddenly thrust open and about a score of Turkish guards came in with buckets of watery stew and black bread. We strongly suspected the ingredients of that stew, but grabbed our portions readily enough. A number of Arabs came in, too, peddling cigarettes, dates, oranges, pomegranates. They were still prepared to accept our *rupees*—providing we gave them enough in exchange for their wares. About forty *rupees* would buy a box of twelve Turkish cigarettes, ten *rupees* for an orange or a handful of dates, and so on. The *rupee* was at that time equivalent to a shilling and three or four coppers, or about a quarter of a dollar.

An old Arab sidled up to us and indicated in a whisper that he recognised Steve's American accent. We stared at the greybeard for a minute. His broken English had a definite American accent!

145

"You have dollars, eh? I bring *arrack!*"

It transpired that he was an Arab seaman. He had come up the Tigris in a Turkish steamer and could not get down to the Persian Gulf again owing to the blockade put across the river below Kut by the British soldiers. He had shipped in cargo steamers all over the world, knew Galveston, New York, Boston, Montreal, Cardiff, the London River. He was a distinct find! He made it perfectly clear that he knew the world value of dollars. Besides he had no time for the Turks. They had robbed him of his job, his possessions, left him stranded. His English cuss-words had a decided tang of the sea.

"Ten bucks. I bring big bottle. So!"

By the way he held his hands one could only assume he meant about ten gallons. Possibly he was exaggerating a little.

"Five bucks," said Steve.

"Five bucks you—five bucks *arrack* for guard. You give ten bucks, eh?"

"All right, sailor! You bring *arrack* first!"

"You have ten bucks? Show me! I bring 'em *arrack!*"

Steve fished two five-dollar bills out of his shoe, rustled them before the Arab, and stowed them back again. The old man turned abruptly, and without a word strode out of the building.

"Was that wise?"

"Showing him the dough? I guess so. The old *wallah's* on the level. If he ain't, I've lost two bucks, for he'll sure tell the guards."

"All you have?"

"Not on your sweet life, Tiger. All I got in my shoe. There's plenty more. I ain't been able to spend a dime since I came with this outfit. First time I've seen an Arab who knew what a dollar was, anyway."

"He certainly does."

"And he may be useful. Help us to make a getaway, maybe."

"How?"

"I guess we could do a lot in a place like Baghdad—with some Arab clobber."

"I fancy there are a great many people hiding in these old buildings."

"You said it, Tiger. If the old guy does come back with the liquor, maybe we could talk to him."

He came within the hour, bringing a large stone bottle of *arrack* in a wicker case. It wasn't quite so big as he had indicated, but it must have held two or three gallons—enough to make a decent-sized party drunk. The party in our corner soon got that way, including quite a number of the women. I suspect that none of us were in much of a condition to withstand the potent spirit.

"Where did you find it?" queried Steve.

"I make him," grinned the Arab. "Good, eh?"

"Damned good! Say! How long do we stay here?"

The old man shrugged his shoulders.

"Maybe one day, maybe two-three days."

"And after that?"

"Other prisoners go Mosul. You go Mosul maybe."

"You come here tomorrow?"

"You got more dollars in other shoe?" grinned the old man.

"Come tomorrow and see!"

Our benefactor disappeared. We set to work on the stone jar. In a little while we were the happiest prisoners in the whole of Mesopotamia! As the fiery spirit distilled from dates began to course madly round our starved innards, we began to act in like manner. Carousal was hardly the word. We sang, danced, fought each other, wrestled, rolled about the floor, scattering frightened women and children, and generally playing the fool. The spirit stirred up an intense desire for the craziest activity, or it may have been a reaction after the depression of past months. Probably both. The vaulted roof echoed and re-echoed our wild singing. Once the guards strode in and attempted to quieten us, but we proved too many for them. They retired, cursing the English, convinced that the long marches had driven us all insane, otherwise how could we sing in such conditions?

But sing we did. We kept it up for hours. One of the boys picked up, with surprising strength, a woman as big as himself, and began to dance around the floor with her, yelling above her screams a popular song of the day:

Oh, you bee-oo-tiful doll,
You great big,—big, bee-oo-tiful doll!
I could never live without you!
I'd like to throw my arms about you!
Oh, you great big,—big, bee-oo-tiful doll!

Nothing could have been less like a beautiful doll than that poor haggard wretch in rags. Not that anybody noticed such things at the time. The chorus was taken up and we grabbed at the nearest woman, girl, child—or bosom pal; and shook the roof. Soon the sober members were singing as crazily as the rest of us. We must have presented an amazing scene, dancing and yelling around that church. We staggered and stumbled around in semi-darkness, for there was little to light up the lurid scene, save the few tiny oil trays that the Armenians had lighted.

One chorus followed another. Women wept. Children wept. I don't know whether from relief or fear. Had the English soldiers gone mad? Or was this the way of English soldiers?

The guards came in again and gazed in wondering amazement. Were the mad English chanting a hymn of peace or celebrating some victory of which they had not heard? No people would kick up such a hullabaloo without sufficient good reason! This Armenian church was the church of the English *nasrani*, too. Obviously we were indulging in some religious rite. They spat contemptuously and left us to our wild orgy of song and dance.

It went on far into the night. It was still going on, less boisterously perhaps, when I dropped to the floor exhausted and slept the sleep of the paralytic drunk.

Most of us had to be clubbed into wakefulness. We were on the move again. Once more we limped through the streets of Baghdad. We needed no one to tell us where we were going—Mosul, of course. Where else could it be? Perhaps Johnny was afraid that the British Army might advance upon Baghdad one of these fine days, and he was making sure of his prisoners.

"If we hadn't indulged in that damned *arrack*, we might have done something with that old Arab *wallah* last night."

"Yeah. Sure, Tiger. There always seems to be an 'if' about our getaways. One time it's women. Then it's liquor. Ain't those two things the ruination of man?"

"You'd make a joke out of a funeral. . . ."

"S'long as it ain't mine!"

"There won't be much chance of escape in Mosul."

"Got a hangover, ain't you? Too bad. Quit worrying, Tiger. I'll bring you back to Baghdad one of these days."

"Don't understand why you wouldn't demand to see your compatriot, the American Consul, when we arrived yesterday. You're a queer cuss, Steve!"

"Yeah," he grinned. "I guess so. British soldier, ain't I? What'n hell do I want to go mewling to the consul for? Guess, I'll make my own way out o' this."

"He could have wangled it so you'd be kept in Baghdad."

But that was as far as he would ever go on the subject. That jaw of his could shut like a clam at times. Had he taken that way out—always supposing it were possible—I fancy I should have been the loneliest soul in the world.

Tiger, then a little short of eighteen, would never have survived.

But lady luck was with us on this trip, at least, for a little while. Batches of us were packed into railway trucks and away we went. I slept most of the way to Samarra—a matter of seventy miles or so from Baghdad. All I can remember of that god-forsaken spot is a great spiral tower, rearing up into the sky several hundreds of feet, said to be built by Alexander the Great as a watch tower. It is detached from the little square, walled town of Samarra and can be seen many miles away. It must command an extraordinary view of the vast sanded plains all around. That tower marked the beginning of as terrible a desert trek as any man could experience. Here the railroad came to a dead stop in the middle of the desert. We now had to walk. We did not know then that Mosul was to be a mere step in the long trek.

General Townshend refers to this historic trek in his work, *My Campaign in Mesopotamia*:

> Anyone who has travelled over the road from Baghdad to Afion Kara Hissar, in Asia Minor, and remembers that our soldiers, worn out and emaciated at the fall of Kut, had to *walk* it, will not wonder that numbers died—the bulk of dysentery.

And again:

> The Turkish line of communications from Constantinople to Baghdad *via* Mosul . . . is some 1,255 miles. It runs from Baghdad *via* Mosul, Ras-al-Ain, Aleppo, Tarsus, over the Taurus Mountains, Bozanti, Konia, and Afion Kara Hissar to Constantinople.

The British Parliamentary report, dry, official language though it may be, is worth quoting at this juncture:

> Their state of preparation for a march of five hundred miles, the health and strength and equipment which they possessed for withstanding one of the fiercest summers of the globe, can be pictured from what has been described already; and the efficiency of the Oriental care to which they were entrusted is as easily imagined. The officers who were left in Baghdad, and

who watched them depart, could only feel the deepest anxiety and dread.

The truth of what happened has only very gradually become known, and in all details it will never be known, for those who could tell the worst are long dead. But it is certain that this desert journey rests upon those responsible for it as a crime of the kind which we call historic, so long and terrible was the torture it meant for thousands of helpless men. If it is urged that Turkish powers of organisation and forethought were utterly incapable of handling such a problem as the transport of these prisoners, the plea is sound enough as an explanation; as an excuse it is nothing.

There was no one in the higher Turkish command who could be ignorant that to send the men out on such a journey and in such conditions was to condemn half of them to certain death, unless every precaution were taken. And there were precautions which were easy and obvious, the chief one being that the prisoners should not be deprived of the care for their health which their own officers could give them. Yet even this plain opportunity was sacrificed, as we have seen, with perfect indifference to the fate of the mere rank and file. Here, as always, we find that Turkish apathy is not as simple as it seems; it betrays considerable respect of persons, and it contrives to evade the most dangerous witnesses of its guilt.

These officers of all ranks, from generals to subalterns, who watched us depart from Baghdad, should have heard the comments of the rank and file! It is true that some of them insisted upon following us as far as Samarra—which was as far as the railway ran—and that they were able to rescue a number of sick men who fell out soon after the march from Samarra had started. But the long and terrible trek had only just begun for the thousands of helpless soldiers! It was known that we left five hundred sick in Baghdad. But how much is known of the hundreds who were left by the wayside, many of them kicked or bludgeoned to death in the very act of dysentery stools?

Nothing can alter the fact that those British officers did leave the rank and file to their fate.

My fleeting glimpse of the town of Mosul gave me an impression of dirt, decrepitude and decay. It stands on the right bank of the Tigris and about 200 miles from Baghdad—a road of horrible memory

SAMARRA, ASSOCIATED BY TRADITION WITH THE STORY OF THE GOOD SAMARITAN.
IN THE FOREGROUND IS THE FAMPUS SPIRAL TOWER

marked out by the skeleton bones of British lads, a road and a trek that I shall not attempt to describe, because if I do I shall be accused of reiterating my tales of atrocity, mutilation and bestiality. I will say only this. Our condition was such during the last few miles of that trek that we could pass indifferently the brown women already at their fiendish work on our comrades. It was enough for the remainder of us to keep on our feet at all by that time.

I recall the crumbling walls and the general air of dilapidation and remember how fitting it should be as a halt for an army of men slowly being done to death. There was a minaret there that stands out like the Leaning Tower of Pisa. One later learned that Moslems believed the minaret to have bowed its head to Mahomet when he passed this way on his celestial flight. It is therefore a matter for astonishment that the minaret did not break its back in bowing over the hundreds of British boys who passed this way on *their* celestial flight.

We left many more at Mosul. In a column more dead than alive, those who could not get to their feet again were left where they had dropped when the column halted and fell in heaps to sleep. It is with no desire to make the reader's flesh creep that I state we then started on another two hundred miles or so across desert and pebbly track to Ras-al-Ain. The fact is on record. We had by no means reached the end of our journey.

The trek from Mosul to Ras-al-Ain is a blurred memory, a distortion of days and nights, of an aching body, an alien mind, of feet like great puddings, every step torture, dragging on and on . . . I don't know to this day how I kept it up. I went through that hell of trudging like a man in a trance . . . the voice of Steve Barry saying things to me as from a great distance. And sometimes he carried me bodily—that man of iron constitution and granite will power.

A strange epoch in the life of young Tiger. A passing through villages of the dead, where hundreds of Armenians and other "Christian dogs" had been violated and slain . . . stench of decaying bodies, grunts and snarls of pariah dogs and jackals at their gluttonous feasts. . . . We looked on. . . . Passed by. . . . Feeling nothing. . . .

"You damned little mutt! D'ya *want* to die!"

Of course I wanted to die. What was there to live for in this mad world that reeked of death and decay—where one caught sight of rabid mongrels tearing at the throats of dead men, where village boundaries were marked by the crucified figures of half-naked girls?

I reached Ras-al-Ain with my nerves in shreds. Malaria took possession of me. It is difficult to record just what happened immediately following our arrival. I was conscious only of a racking fever, a temperature that threatened to burst the temples. One's head became an engine of torture. The body was burning up. So much of my own physical condition was colouring mind and thought that it was impossible to differentiate between the wild chaos of dreams and the stark dreadfulness of realities.

It may have gone on for a few days or a few weeks. I cannot remember. But dear old Steve was still there when I began to sit up and take notice. I was in a shed with scores of others, British and Indian, and Steve was ministering to me like an angel. He looked like one. The fellow was clean, almost, one might say, spruce! He had remained behind with me. I never knew how he wangled it. He just wouldn't talk about it. But I can imagine what happened when he began to tell the Turkish officers "where they got off." Anyway, there he was, having bathed and refreshed and cleaned himself generally in between whiles of nursing and bathing me and bringing down a maddening temperature. He swore his only method was water—constant applications of it inside and outside.

Returning to consciousness is, in any circumstances, a period of strange sensations. One's mind is seething with thoughts at once hideous and ludicrous. One comes gradually to the realities of things. That hand clutching at something which dripped cold water quite fascinated my waking moments. How soothing this cold water! I lay in a blanket drenched with cold water. Cold water was running from my face, streaming over my naked body. Oh, soothing cold, cold water!

There can be no relief like the passing of an abnormally high temperature. It means the passing of terrible dreams. In those dreams I had been a prisoner in the hands of the enemy. I was being tortured with hot bayonets. I was bound head, hand and foot, but more especially head—with a binding that seemed to be crushing the skull to pulp. I was in an Arab encampment. Fires of huge palms burned all around me and the heat was terrific. On the outer circle of the flames danced native girls in robes whose chief colours appeared to be fiery red! Burning tissues! Riotous workings of the mind!

And then that hand dripping cool water! One's eyes opened wide to the fact that Steve's grinning jowl was clean—clean, as if newly washed! It seemed incredible. Then it all came back with a rush. The nightmare days of shuffling through the dirt.

"How d'ya feel, Tiger?"

"Fine! Where are we now?"

"In Ras-al-Ain. This is the railhead from Aleppo. We've covered nearly four hundred miles since we left Samarra a month ago. Most of the column has gone on by rail. A bunch of Indians has been kept back here to work on the railroad extension. But no British—except the sick. So we'll have a bit of railroad travelling when we get going again. How's that?"

"Sounds fine!"

The rail journey that carried us out of Ras-al-Ain was a curious one for me. One does not get much of a view of the landscape from a railroad truck. I did not know what the country through which we passed was like, nor care. Steve had procured a bottle of *arrack* before we started, and the weirdest collection of fruits from dates to melons. On this strange diet I dozed and slept most of the way. Perhaps it was as good a diet as one could have in that climate and under those conditions. There were ration biscuits, too, which I chewed when half-asleep. I actually put on flesh. Army biscuits, if taken regularly, can be quite fattening.

But Aleppo was not for us! We spent several hours on the outskirts while our trucks were shunted around. Then off we went again. At that time the railway ended at Islaheya. And that was where our truck-riding ended for the time being. We were handed over to a fresh lot of guards and marched away to prison camps.

These guards were a particularly brutal lot. Steve and I went through the same pantomime regarding our now-ragged officer's uniform. The swine did not know quite what to do about us. Eventually they decided to club us in with the rest and take a chance.

In a few hours we were hot-footing again. As I recall it, it was not a very long journey, but it was damnably hard going over broken country. We forded streams, straggled along hillsides, stumbled over scrub, beat it along a lowering valley where the air was chilled and damp. In the distance, mountains—but they were in the distance! Never meet troubles half-way! Steve and I were fit enough then as a result of our rest and rail journey. But that could not be said for a lot of the poor devils.

These guards did not seem to realise that their brethren on the other side of Asia Minor had very nearly thrashed us to a standstill. They used their rifle-butts unmercifully. Over that broken road we left another trail of dead and dying. One wondered how many of the tragically thin column would be left to tell the tale by the time these sadistic brutes of Turkey had finished driving us like cattle across this wild country.

We came at long last to another railhead, where railroad construction was proceeding apace. (At least we had a glimpse of Kaiser Wilhelm's dream of a railroad from Berlin to Baghdad—that is, the handful of us who came out of that historic trek.)

And then they put us to work on the railway! Most of the mob were incapable of lifting a sleeper or shoving a line of steel into position. So they were tied up and flogged until their insensible bodies were reduced to bleeding pulp, just as an example to others. Fortunately, we had not yet reached the end of our journey! The bulk of us were moved on—a short journey by rail to Adana, where the railroad came to a dead stop again!

CHAPTER 14

Escape!

Then we became mountain goats—treading a bleeding path over the Taurus Mountains, for the ambitious Berlin-to-Baghdad railway had not then been cut through the great mountain passes of Asia Minor. This was the last stage of the great trek to the Turkish prison camp of ill fame at Afion Kara Hissar, in Anatolia. Seven hundred British soldiers died or were killed during that march over the Taurus range. Some of them just lay down and died, especially the Indian units, for the simple and all-sufficing reason that they could do nothing else.

Climbing the mountain paths brought grand opportunities for the exercising of Johnny Turk's sense of humour. Weaklings who would insist on straggling behind were eliminated by the simple process of jabbing them in the tummy and sending them head over heels on to the sharp crags below.

No. I am not beginning another account of Turkish brutalities and atrocities. Enough has now been given to show why more than seventy per cent of the original twelve thousand who left Kut as Turkish prisoners of war in May, 1916, are now nothing but calcined bones marking the long and tragic road from Mesopotamia to Anatolia.

Those who wish to continue the tale of cruelties and barbarities, inflicted upon the last remnants of the Kut garrison of Afion Kara Hissar, must seek other sources of information. They will learn how the daily floggings and nightly pederastic indulgences of the commandant and his henchmen finally reached the ears of the horrified American consuls in certain Anatolian centres. And then the Turkish Government *had* to sit up and take notice.

No. I'm through. After deliberating for years over this closing phase of a chronicle that has not been easy to set down, I have to conclude that I am incapable of detailing the life of the Kut remnants at Afion

Kara Hissar. Moreover, Steve and I tolerated it for only a little while. Escape had never been out of our minds throughout that ghostly march. The summer was advancing and we knew we must make a getaway soon, since the winter snows of those regions would make the journey to the coast quite impossible.

That was the scheme outlined by my friend. We must escape and make our way down to the coast. The trek to Mersina would be a mere trifle compared to what we had gone through during the past months. Besides, it meant freedom! We were determined to try it. It might mean the end of us. But what other prospect was there in Afion Kara Hissar? On the other hand, there was the possibility that we should make the port. We could then get a neutral ship to Cyprus, or even to Port Said. What was to happen afterwards we could well leave the future to decide. The thing that occupied our minds was the manner of escaping. We did not care what happened, so long as we could get away from the madman at Afion Kara Hissar. No life could possibly be worse than this! The future was on the knees of the gods.

"I was a sailor before I was a soldier, Tiger. I guess I can do it again. And so can you! And you can take it from me—good American dollars will get us anywhere!"

They certainly got us civilian clothes and strong, thick greatcoats, for, like the rest of the men of Kut, we still wore the rags of summer drill cloth that had clothed us when we started to march as prisoners, and now the days were cooler, the nights perishing cold, and we had not known the rigours of a winter climate for more than two years.

We heard other men discussing the chances of escape, but we said not a word about our preparations. Naturally most of the boys were disheartened, weak from privation, without the will to carry out their schemes. Some talked despondently of the uselessness of trying to reach the coast. The region was mountainous—as if we had not already marched over mountains! We should need to make a detour of nearly two hundred miles—as if we had not already hardened ourselves to treks of hundreds of miles! We should meet with bands of brigands known to be infesting the country—as if any brigands in the world could be worse than our jailers! And what about food?

Food was always in Tommy's mind. So little ever found its way into his tummy. But we had learned to scramble along on the strangest of diets. Neither Steve nor I felt any fear on this score. Nor should we have any scruples. We should go as freebooters, living on the country, taking what we could, when and how we could. To us, it was a glorious prospect! If we died from hunger in the mountains—well, so be it.

We had travelled more than fifteen hundred miles since that day, long, long ago, when we landed at Fao Fort in the Persian Gulf! Should we worry about a couple of hundred miles that meant freedom?

And then something happened that changed our plans entirely. Parties of more or less fit men were sent to the railroad to load trucks with guns and munitions for the Mesopotamian front! This was the final irony! Another example of Johnny's sense of humour. We had to work like galley slaves loading material that was to be used later to blow British soldiers to blazes, while guards stood around with whips and guns and grinned.

It took Steve and myself about two seconds to see the possibilities in this spot of fatigue!

"Ever jumped the rods, Tiger?"

"You mean ridden under a train? No. But I'm game!"

"Great fellah! Listen! This job may last some time. There is a chance we could get a train going back the way we came. Get me? We could travel by the railroad as far as the railhead at Dorak, but instead of carrying on over the mountains, the way we came, we'd turn south for the coast. That may be a mountainous route too, but it ain't many miles to the coast from the railhead and we'd make it in a few hours. That part's easy enough. The big job is getting our stuff down here and then getting the train."

"We could bring our civilian clothes here a piece at a time and hide them. When we have them assembled in some place, we'll grab them and jump for a train going east!"

"Yeah. But how are we to get the clobber here?"

"Wear it under these clothes. We'll look a bit fatter. But still. . . ."

"And the greatcoats?"

"Wear them. Make an excuse about the weather getting colder here. Can't stand it after the heat."

As we worked, Steve contrived to instruct me, without being observed, regarding the underworks of a railroad truck. He showed me the rod to grip with my hands, how to wrap my legs around the supports and rest my back. I wondered how far I could travel while slung under a truck in that fashion. I was as excited as a school kid at the idea of this venture for freedom, and ready for anything.

"Some fellows can do hundreds of miles that way. But I doubt if you'd stick long, Tiger. Don't worry about that. As soon as we get clear of this place we'll climb into a truck and ride more comfortably. Get me? But, remember! There'll be guards riding the trucks!"

"Will they be on every truck?"

"I guess so. Maybe a couple of men on each one."

"We'll take the place of two of them!"

"Say! How d'ya get this way, Tiger!"

"A bid for freedom, by God! Would we stop at knocking a couple of guards out and taking their place complete with coats, caps and guns?"

"I should say not! Say! That's an idea! We won't rouse any suspicion by wearing our greatcoats. Go without them. If we are to nobble a couple of guards. . . . !"

And that, for once in this tale of ill luck, was how it worked out. On the third day of our fatigue at the railroad everything was ready. When the men were lined up at dusk for the march back to quarters, Steve and I were missing. As we suspected, nobody troubled. Men were often missing. We were then lying side by side under a truck. I don't know how men manage to hold that torturous position for hundreds of miles, or if they ever do. All I know is that by the time the train had started I was just about ready to relax my grip and let go!

It seemed that we lay in that position for hours before the train began to move. My muscles were stiff and aching intolerably with the strain. Cramp was playing the devil with my legs, raising great knots of muscle and giving one excruciating pains. I could have yelled with relief when those wheels started to turn.

"Hang on for a little while longer!" shouted Steve, above the rattle of axles and the rumble of wheels.

"Can't!" I yelled back.

"All right! Watch me. Make every move as I do, or you'll be killed, you little mutt!"

Slowly we worked our way to the end of the truck.

Luckily the train had not yet gathered speed. I followed and copied each move Steve made with straining eyes and bulging muscles. The sweat began to pour. I was not afraid. But I was fully aware of what a false move on my part would mean!

"When you get your legs round the buffer, stay put till I can give you a hand!"

I hung on with my hands, my face within a few inches of the underside of the truck, my feet groping round the edge of the structure until I felt the smooth surface of the buffer barrel, then wrapped my legs about it and waited. In the dimness of that strange rumbling world I watched Steve at work. I had a strange feeling of confidence from then onwards, a feeling of elation at everything we did. I knew, as certain as I'd ever known anything, that we should get through!

Steve disappeared round the edge of the truck. I gathered he had heaved himself on to the buffer. He certainly wasn't on the track! Presently his voice came down to me.

"Can you see my hand?"

"Sure!"

"All right. Hang on like hell with your legs! Let go with one hand and grab mine! Good! Now the other hand! Steady! Up you come, old fellah!"

"I'm sitting astride the buffer with my nose bumping into the truck. What do I do next?"

"You learn to keep your balance, you little runt! I want to take my hand off your shoulders. D'ya think I can hold you here all night?"

"All right. You can let go!"

"Sure?"

"Of course!"

I hung on to a bar that ran across the flat face of the truck back and decided that the position was as luxurious as an armchair compared to those rods. The train of wagons was gathering speed. It wasn't so comfortable then. As the wheels lifted the points I was lifted clean off the buffer and dropped back again, a performance that soon began to tell on the tender portions of one's anatomy.

"How long do we stick this? Aren't we going to investigate? "

"Hold yourself, Tiger! There's plenty of time! Give these guards a chance and they'll soon be asleep."

"The way I'm being jogged about . . . I'll have no bottom left soon!"

"Think yourself lucky you've got one—and for the love of Pete—don't make a move till I tell you!"

"Where the devil could I go, anyway?"

"Hang on as long as you can, old fellah. I want to give these Johnnies a chance of shut-eye. It'll make the job less risky. Remember, we've gotta crawl over this truck without 'em knowing a thing about it."

I hung on for miles, jogging up and down on an iron horse. If only I'd been a trained cavalryman! . . . The trucks were rolling and lurching at an ever-increasing speed, clattering through the black night at a pace I should hardly have thought possible on such a railway track. Maybe the engine driver was working for a timed arrival at the railhead. Certainly he was carrying a lot of important stores and war material. I had assisted in putting the stuff aboard.

Presently Steve hoisted himself to his feet until he was standing on the buffer. He peered over the top of the truck board. Steve was all of six feet in height, but he could only just see over the great wall of boarding. I wondered what would happen when I tried to climb over—with my five feet, six!

"The truck seems to be full of saddles, equipment and such, and there's two Johnnies stretched out on it, nursing rifles. They may be asleep. Maybe not. Anyway, they can't see much in this blackness. What say?"

"Of course! Let's go to it!"

"All right. Hang on till I get astride the top. Then I'll give you a hand."

I nodded. Steve gripped the top of the board and slowly hoisted himself up. With one leg over the top he reached down to pull me up and alongside. We were both sitting on top of the board and nothing happened. It looked as if those two guards were taking a nap. We could dimly see the outline of their recumbent forms and the glint of rifles. There we stayed for several long minutes.

Then, at an agreed signal from Steve, we dropped on top of them. They didn't have a chance! Even if they had been awake they could not have heard our movements above the rattle and clatter of the lurching trucks. We pounded them with their own guns. After which we set to work removing their coats, ammunition pouches, Mauser pistols, knives, odds and ends of money, cigarettes, and other useful articles. Each had a canvas pouch full of rations for the journey and a water bottle filled not with water but *arrack!* We were in clover!

It was with enormous feelings of satisfaction that we heaved the insensible Johnnies over the side of the truck and sent them tumbling on to the track. We hoped they would get run over by the next train. We might have finished them altogether, but they were not worth the trouble. All we wanted was to be rid of them. Brethren of this kidney had slaughtered hundreds of our comrades in cold blood and often in the most beastly fashion. One has to experience that sort of thing day after day, week in and week out, month after month, in order fully to appreciate what we felt when we chucked those fellows over the side! Had we been given to bestial practices we might have done much more to the carrion. We were not built that way!

Thereafter a feast for the gods! We investigated the canvas pouches. There was bread of a quality we had not tasted in years, succulent goat's meat, olives, radishes, figs, dates and some sticky sweetmeat. It all went down with tremendous relish! We drank sparingly of the *arrack*. We should yet need all our wits. Besides, it would serve us in good stead later, when, peradventure, food was not easy to come by. Then we lay back in the truck and inhaled luxuriously at the cigarettes! That was a moment worth striving for. Just then we were sitting on top of the world, not on top of a German-built truck full of Turkish military stores.

Not for many months had we been able to relax! Every waking hour had found us on the alert, on the defensive against the jailer's club or rifle-butt, on watch for the slightest chance of escaping; and that sort of strain tells on a man sooner or later. How can I describe all we felt in those sweet moments of relaxation? This was not a lumbering railroad truck swaying through the sullen night. It was a limousine of upholstered ease gliding through a night of dreams to freedom!

Freedom! For the first time in years my heart sang! We were free! *Free!* True, we were not yet out of the danger zone, but I never felt so confident of success in my life. After all we had gone through, every breath we now took was a taste of heaven. It was good to be alive. The very night air whistling around our heads was sharp, bracing, invigorating! No heat, no dust, no parching thirst, no stench, no Arab familiar!

"Guess one of us had better get some shut-eye. We'll need all the strength we've got later on. Supposing you kip down, Tiger, while I keep guard? I'll waken you in a couple of hours."

"Nothing doing, Steve. I couldn't sleep just now if I tried. Never was so wide awake in my life! Can't imagine how anybody could want to sleep after an experience like this!"

"Nope? Watch me! Right now I could sleep on a tight-rope. I'll leave you to keep watch, but if you feel drowsy, kid, waken me up at once. It would be disastrous if we both fell asleep. Get me?"

"All right, Steve. I promise."

In two minutes Steve was snoring fit to beat the band. I sat and listened, reclining with my head against a saddle, staring up at the blue-black canopy of heaven. I have never experienced anything like that strange night. I doubt if I ever shall again. I was soon lost in a dream world of my own. I forgot Steve, forgot everything. I was at home in the green lanes of Surrey, strolling through a night of perfect peace, where there were neither thoughts of war nor sounds of strife, where only stability and serenity was, where there was security and peace for a troubled soul.

My heart sang to the rhythm of the revolving wheels. There was only me in that blue-black world of motion. I had been set free from a long, long nightmare of horrors. Every turn of these chanting wheels took me nearer to the beautiful things of life that had been shut out for two dreadful years. I dreamed of green fields drenched in soft-falling rain, of the countryside turned golden-brown in autumn, of an English snow-white Christmas, the cosy warmth of a log fire, homely cottage scenes, simple, peaceful country life—such glorious pictures passing in grand procession across the delicate texture of the mind.

I was going home. I knew I was going home! Please, God!

It was all so clear to me, just what I must do. We should reach Port Said, Steve and I. We could report to the military authorities there. They could hardly do other than send us to England. I would show this hard-bitten, mosquito-salted, world-wandering friend of mine what it meant to be home. Home! Lord of the living! What a world of meaning in that simple phrase!

Gradually I became conscious of the changing atmosphere about me. The lowering darkness that had enveloped me utterly seemed lifting. The change broke through my absorption. The dark vault overhead was softening. There came a faint flush of colour. I sat up with a jerk. It seemed I had daydreamed through the night.

My sudden movement woke Steve with a jerk. He sat up, awake on the instant, stared around, swore.

"The dawn's coming up. You've let me sleep all night! What the hell—!"

"It's been a marvellous night!" said I.

"Tiger! You're more screwy than I thought you were! You get down to it right now. You'll need it. Ain't you learned yet how to reserve your forces? Come on! Kip down, and stop playing the damned fool!"

I slept, remembering nothing, seeing nothing during the next few hours. When I awoke the sun was high in the heavens. The morning hours were passing. Steve was crouched by the side of the truck, looking like a pukkah Turkish guard in the coat and cap with the barrel of his rifle sticking over the truck rail.

"So far, so good. We ain't stopped any place yet. I've seen no sign of the other guards. Never a glimpse of the brigands or Arab looters, and we've passed through some queer country, I can tell you! Now we've got to keep our eyes skinned. It may be that this train is going to run through every station and not stop at all till she gets to the railhead. But, I guess that's too good to be true. We'll see!"

"What do we do if she pulls up at a station?"

"Guess I ain't thought that one out. If we do stop, some *wallah*, an officer or an N.C.O., is going to run along the trucks and see that all's correct."

"He wouldn't know us from the real article if we kept our coats buttoned and caps pulled down."

"Is that so? Go on, tell me the Turkish lingo for—All correct, sir!"

"Supposing we wait and see whether she stops?"

"You said all that's in my mind, Tiger. I ain't leaving this truck while she keeps on drawing me away from Afion-Kara-Kisser! Not me! If we'd chosen our own train we couldn't have done better than this! Seems like Johnny is crying out for shells and such. I wonder if he's still got Kut?"

"The hot season is over now in Messup. That means Johnny is fighting like hell to keep what he's got."

"Yeah. I say! These Turkey guards don't fraternise much. Nobody's yelled good morning to us yet."

"A mixed unit, I suppose—Germans and Turks. From what I've seen of them, Jerry don't seem to like Johnny very much."

"Maybe something in that. How about your German lingo—supposing we get in a jam at one of the stations?"

"Good enough for a Turkish officer."

"Gosh! Then why worry!"

"Is it worth the risk—now we've got so far? There's covered trucks in front of the train and some at the tail, and you can bet your boots they're full of Turkish soldiers. If we stop for any length of time at a station, these fellows may not recognise us as good comrades! "

"I guess you're right, Tiger. If she shows signs of stopping any station, we'll jump for it."

The train went on hour after hour. We passed villages, one or two military camps, an occasional dump, careered along country that showed no sign of life for mile upon mile, barren, rock-strewn country. It was well past noon when we sighted the distant outline of what appeared to be a large town. We drew nearer, came upon cultivated fields, farmsteads, hamlets, all the signs of approach to a town of some importance. But the train showed no signs of slowing up for a halt. The features of the town took shape, became familiar. One remembered passing this way under guard. It was Konieh! We recognised the ruined monastery, the mosques, the sacred tombs. Here, according to tradition, was the very heart and centre of the dancing dervishes in the Ottoman Empire.

Konieh was the most important town on that stretch of the railroad. We gathered together the Mauser pistols and the water bottles—having no use for the rifles or the empty pouches—but the train showed no sign of stopping. We hung on, suffering agonies of indecision. We could detect no slackening of the speed. This was no place to disembark! If we jumped and then found the train wasn't stopping. . . . The buildings loomed up large and impressive. It became too late to jump. We dared not drop into this town. Discovery was almost certain. We should be thrown to the mob! I experienced moments of real terror when, approaching the station, the train slackened her pace. . . . But she went through! I wiped the sweat from my face and stared with immense relief at the fast-disappearing buildings. The train was gathering speed again.

I stared at Steve. He grinned. I could have danced! Lady Luck was still with us. We had passed the most important station on the line! Now there was no likelihood of our stopping before we reached the railhead! We knew we had covered more than two-thirds of the track. The day was waning. Just how long would it take us to make the remainder of this trip? It could only be a matter of hours at this speed. We calculated that we should reach our destination before the dawn of another day. Nothing would suit us better. To arrive during the night or early morning would give us excellent cover for the getaway.

Darkness descended and we settled down, taking guard by turns. But this second night brought no fanciful dreams. I was far too excited now to do anything but crawl over that wagon and stare into the black night. The next big test would soon be upon us. When my turn for rest came I could not rest. Sleep was impossible. In spite of all my experiences—or perhaps because of them!—I was more jumpy than I had ever been. As for my companion, nothing seemed to disturb that hard-boiled *wallah*. He would snuggle down for his rest and be asleep in a matter of seconds. When he was wakened he was really awake, instantly alert! He could get down to it and up again with the precision of a clock. Maybe the sea had done that for him.

It was during the early hours of the morning that the train began to slow down. There was no mistaking her intention this time. We did not wait for her to stop. The wink and flash of lights ahead was warning enough. We jumped, lay still while the train of wagons drew past us, then got to our feet and stumbled across the track to the outer darkness.

We had no clear idea then as to the direction we were taking. We knew vaguely that by moving off at right-angles to the railroad track we should make southwards. All that was necessary then was to get away from the railhead and all that it stood for, away into the blackness, away from any sign of human habitation. We staggered on, saying nothing, since our footsteps made noise enough.

It was a weird progress we made, moving more or less blindly into the darkness. Anon we would turn about and check direction by the distant lights that marked the railhead. It still wanted a couple of hours to dawn. Once we pulled up sharply. Light appeared ahead of us. We continued again—cautiously. To turn back was out of the question. We just had to see what this light ahead of us meant. It grew larger. It was low on the ground.

"Camp fire!" snapped Steve. "Military camp. Prowling sentries. Keep your lights skinned, Tiger!"

We crawled like cats. Soon we were near enough to mark the outline of the camp. Figures passed back and forth in the light of the fires. It was not a very large camp. There were some thirty or forty tents, horse lines, gun limbers. Obviously an outpost for the railhead. It was a thousand miles from the fighting line in Mesopotamia, but in this area of brigands the post was probably a very necessary precaution.

There was nothing for it but to make a wide detour. Even if we missed direction we must give the place a wide berth before the dawn light came up! We went, crunching a gravel trail, trying to step noiselessly and speedily. As the lights grew dim to the left of us we began to double. Then we found ourselves dipping into a gully. An hour passed, still we plodded on. We lost sight of the camp fires. We kept moving until the first streak of dawn showed us that our detour had put us sadly out of direction. We sat down and waited for daylight. Soon the whole world was lit up with the flush of a new day.

And what a wilderness! An undulating expanse of gravelly ground and away in the distance rolling hills. Not a vestige of life anywhere. Bleak desolation met the eye. For breakfast we had *arrack* and cigarettes. It seemed somehow to be in keeping with the drab landscape. We corrected our direction by the position of the rising sun, jumped

A LATER VIEW OF MOSUL
SHOWING NATIVE LIFE IN THE BAZAAR

to our feet and started off at the double. We kept that pace for nearly two hours—then the effects of the *arrack* wore off and we broke into a walk-march!

Steve was of the opinion that we should make the coast before nightfall if we could manage to keep going all day. By noon we had left the wilderness behind and were climbing over hilly ground, dipping into valleys, careering up hill and down dale in a mad thrust towards the sea.

I cannot recall the number of villages and hamlets we passed during that long day from dawn until sunset. I know only that Steve insisted on going forward when I would have given anything to lie down and rest. We emptied the *arrack* and filled up with water at a stream, picked some sort of a turnip-root from a field and fed as we tramped along. Once we came upon a band of men and women, dragging donkeys and goats. They cast curious glances in our direction, but we could see no sign of anything that looked like a gun, and concluded they were harmless enough. We traded our knives for bread, using the universal language of signs and gestures, for their tongue was entirely foreign to us. Cilicians, we concluded, and passed on.

Then came a long trail through a wooded pass in the mountains, and we came at last to look down upon the little seaport. The sun was beginning to dip over the distant water. I shall never forget that picture as long as I live. There was the Mediterranean! The sun was turning the blue to gold for our especial benefit. It was a perfect eye-salve for us tired and weary souls. I wanted to sit down and blubber like a child. The Turkish swine would not get us now. We had beaten them—by God!

"Steve!" I cried. "You said you'd do it!"

Try as I would, I couldn't stop my eyes filling with tears. Steve saw—and looked away.

"Sure, old fellah! We've got a few miles to tramp yet, but the end's in sight. Now we come to the easiest part. I guess I know enough about ships to get me out of any seaport in the world! Come on, Tiger! Step on it!"

CHAPTER 15

Steve Says Goodbye

Steve was as good as his word. We got under cover in that little seaport town for a while and presently emerged in the rig common to trampship fo'c'sle hands. There was no fear of our being detected, however. Steve *was* an American seaman. He required no disguise. For my part, I was content to play follow-my-leader. We moved about the place freely enough—on my pal's good dollars!—fraternised with seamen from every quarter of the globe, made a corner for ourselves in the usual dives, and almost forgot during two joyous months of freedom that we'd ever been soldiers in the British Army!

Kut, Ctesiphon Arch, Baghdad, Mosul, Ras-al-Ain, Aleppo, Afion Kara Hissar—what were these but names of places vaguely remembered by two freely-roving Yankee seamen! We caroused to our heart's content. We went into forbidden places, supped, and chose the one we loved best, and knew dimly that somewhere there was a terrible war going on. But we felt we had earned this little respite. When our money gave out we traded our Mausers and cartridges, and caroused some more. Between whiles Steve would lead me down to the ships, look them over with a nautical eye and declare there was nothing there for us!

"There's plenty of time, Tiger! Plenty of time! You've got all your young life before you. What the hell . . .!"

Heaven knows how long we should have stayed in that quiet back-water had it not been for a little episode that very nearly put "paid" to my account. It occurred in a wine shop. The cause of the trouble was a girl with big, dark eyes, luxuriant black tresses, massive gold ear-dangles, attractive contours and a devastating smile.

The witch had parked herself on my knees and was enjoying her-self there when a greasy Levantine rolled up, gave her a dirty look, and addressed certain remarks to me of an unparliamentary nature. I had already put away a fair quantity of cheap wine.

I rose, upsetting the laughing wench, strolled over to the truculent member, and planted a straight left to the point of his jaw. He staggered. He was so astonished that he could only gape for a long minute. That made the assembled men and women roar with laughter. Then he came over like an infuriated bull.

In my fuddled state I did not notice the knife. It was only when I closed with him, felt the vicious jab that ripped open my old shoulder wound, that I realised the seriousness of the situation. Steve plunged and dragged the fellow off by the scruff of the neck, planted another but more powerful one to the point and laid the Levantine flat.

We did what we could with the torn shoulder, but it was a decidedly nasty business. In brief, it began its old tactics of refusing to heal. We lay low for a couple of weeks. It was that which determined me. I decided in no uncertain terms that we should get out of the place without further delay. Steve agreed.

He did more. He got us aboard a Dutch tramp bound for Port Said, himself as a *pukkah* fo'c'sle hand and Tiger as an "extra deckhand at a shilling a month," which is the way of ships, I understand, when carrying a passenger though not licensed to do so. Thereafter a quiet and healing trip across the Mediterranean.

I could not help contrasting this little sea voyage with that other one made more than two years ago, when I came down the Mediterranean in a troopship. I recalled the sunny afternoon when a French torpedo boat came alongside us, her decks all awash, and her skipper yelled through a megaphone to our skipper:

"There are ships under the sea! You are advised to turn back to Algiers."

But we didn't. Not then. The great troopship began to race through the water after the fashion of a destroyer, with every ounce of speed she had. Night came. We stood "at ease" on the decks most of the night, waiting for the order to take to the boats and listening to the zoom and bong of the torpedoes the submarine was trying to plant into us. Next morning we found ourselves in the lovely Bay of Algiers. We had to turn back! When night came we started to run the gauntlet again, and somehow got through.

I felt like an old sailor when I saw the familiar approach to Port Said. I have visited the port many times since those days, but it will always be a source of fascination to me. There came first the lighthouse, then some low-lying land—Damietta, the wide and calm expanse of the outer reaches of the canal mouth.

It was the sort of scene that only the East could evolve. All manner of craft was afloat. There was a big P. and O. liner rigged as a troopship, British and French gunboats, American and other neutral shipping lying-to while native traders in rowing boats bobbed in and out among them. The port literally swarmed with lithe brown figures.

Steve and I stepped into the ship's small launch and were chugged ashore. In a few minutes we were in the thick of it all. I cannot hope to describe that sensation! We sought a *café* and sat where we could gaze on the passing throng—the most vociferous, most colourful, most animated crowd in the world!

"I suppose we'd better find G.H.Q. and report? It will be interesting to see what sort of a reception we shall get!"

"It will be interesting, Tiger, to watch their reactions to our funny story. Remember, we haven't a thing to prove ourselves, except our identity discs."

"And that's enough, surely?"

"I guess so. But it will take 'em about six months to trace our records. They'll wade through files in Whitehall, London, and more files in the Indian Office—and meantime, what happens to us? I'll tell you. We shall be shoved into one of these units here and we'll go on fatigues and squad drills and parades like a couple of blasted recruits."

"Don't you want to report?"

"Not that way. Look here, Tiger, I've got a plan. Let's get across the canal and make our way to Cairo. We've still got a bit of dough. One last fling in that place. And, anyway, it will be a better military centre than this for the next kick off. What say?"

I agreed, but it was not until we had finally reached Cairo that I learned Steve's reason for wanting to get there. In some mysterious way he had heard of a youngster named Lawrence, who was making his presence felt among the military bigwigs of Cairo. All the world now knows of "Lawrence of Arabia." But at that time, early 1917, he was hardly in the spotlight. One gathered that he was trying to persuade the Arabian Bureau of London to support the Arabs of Mecca and Medina in their fight against the Turks. In short, that spot of bother was only just beginning. It looked as if it might be interesting. But at that date no one could have foreseen, not even Lawrence himself, the gigantic drive of the Arabians against the Turks, from the south right through to Damascus!

Just the same, Steve could not resist the urge to get among these independent Arabs in the Hedjas. And there we split. I wanted to see England before I again took up a rifle in this cursed war that appeared to be going on and on indefinitely. I wanted to go home. Apparently Steve knew not the meaning of the word. He was just as determined to carry out his crazy plan of becoming an Arab of the Arabians and getting into the bunch that was scrapping after the fashion of his own heart.

I never heard of such a mad scheme in my life, and said so. Steve just grinned. He went his way. I went mine. Several years were to pass before I should see him again—during a visit to New York. Not until then did I learn that the plan had worked. It was not, after all, quite so crazy as it seemed, when one was made aware of all the circumstances attendant upon that hectic period.

Steve became one of the *Fake Arabs with Lawrence*—but that is another record, which shall be set down in due time.

* 9 7 8 1 7 8 2 8 2 3 3 4 6 *